"This gem of a book sparkles w
Presa points us toward a joy th
gift, a summons and a grace."

—MELANIE C. ROSS, associate professor of liturgical studies, Yale Divinity School

"In this powerful book, Neal Presa offers all who follow Jesus a great gift: the permission to be joyful. Given the weightiness of life's burdens and the injustice of our world, we can easily lose the joy that is to mark discipleship of Jesus. Presa calls us to root our souls in the joy of the Spirit and, through this, to work for peace in the world from the depths of God's sustaining joy."

—JOEL LAWRENCE, executive director, Center for Pastor Theologians

"Encountering this book is to embark on a pilgrimage of joy. Neal Presa reveals how liturgy and worship frame life, with vulnerable stories rooted in his own faithful journey, embedded with rich theological insights. You'll learn the depth of joy from a remarkable church leader. Take and read."

—WES GRANBERG-MICHAELSON, author of
Without Oars: Casting Off into a Life of Pilgrimage

"This book is a deeply necessary journey toward 'joy' as it breathes new perspective on justice and worship. Neal Presa offers us a fresh way to think about Sunday morning worship and calls us to deepen our awareness of communal liturgical practices that reveal God anew. Reading this book moves us to witness God's power at work around us in our fellowship and connection to one another as we worship God together."

—KHALIA J. WILLIAMS, associate dean of worship and spiritual formation, Candler School of Theology, Emory University

"'Joy is elusive. It's like Happiness, but not quite.' Neal Presa writes out of his own experience embedded in his loving family, satisfying work, and professional success, yet finding his heart and soul blocked by tasks, expectations, responsibilities, obligations, and deadlines. This blockage led to 'wrestling' with God and with himself. Presa describes 'a liturgical spirituality' that leads to the One who is our joy and guides us as we learn and embrace hope and justice."

—**Ronald Byars**, professor emeritus of preaching and worship, Union Presbyterian Seminary

WORSHIP, JUSTICE, AND JOY

WORSHIP AND WITNESS

The Worship and Witness series seeks to foster a rich, interdisciplinary conversation on the theology and practice of public worship, a conversation that will be integrative and expansive. Integrative, in that scholars and practitioners from a wide range of disciplines and ecclesial contexts will contribute studies that engage church and academy. Expansive, in that the series will engage voices from the global church and foreground crucial areas of inquiry for the vitality of public worship in the twenty-first century.

The Worship and Witness series demonstrates and cultivates the interaction of topics in worship studies with a range of crucial questions, topics, and insights drawn from other fields. These include the traditional disciplines of theology, history, and pastoral ministry—as well as cultural studies, political theology, spirituality, and music and the arts. The series focus will thus bridge church worship practices and the vital witness these practices nourish.

We are pleased that you have chosen to join us in this conversation, and we look forward to sharing this learning journey with you.

Series Editors:
John D. Witvliet
Noel Snyder
Maria Cornou

WORSHIP, JUSTICE, AND JOY

A Liturgical Pilgrimage

NEAL D. PRESA

Foreword by John D. Witvliet

CASCADE *Books* • Eugene, Oregon

WORSHIP, JUSTICE, AND JOY
A Liturgical Pilgrimage

Worship and Witness

Copyright © 2025 Neal D. Presa. All rights reserved. Except for brief quotations in critical publications or reviews, no part of this book may be reproduced in any manner without prior written permission from the publisher. Write: Permissions, Wipf and Stock Publishers, 199 W. 8th Ave., Suite 3, Eugene, OR 97401.

Cascade Books
An Imprint of Wipf and Stock Publishers
199 W. 8th Ave., Suite 3
Eugene, OR 97401

www.wipfandstock.com

PAPERBACK ISBN: 978-1-6667-3180-4
HARDCOVER ISBN: 978-1-6667-2473-8
EBOOK ISBN: 978-1-6667-2474-5

Cataloguing-in-Publication data:

Names: Presa, Neal D., author. | Witvliet, John D., foreword.

Title: Worship, justice, and joy : a liturgical pilgrimage/ Neal D. Presa; foreword by John D. Witvliet

Description: Eugene, OR: Cascade Books, 2025 | Series: Worship and Witness | Includes bibliographical references.

Identifiers: ISBN 978-1-6667-3180-4 (paperback) | ISBN 978-1-6667-2473-8 (hardcover) | ISBN 978-1-6667-2474-5 (ebook)

Subjects: LCSH: Joy—Religious aspects—Christianity. | Social justice—Religious aspects—Christianity. | Worship.

Classification: BJ1481 P72 2025 (print) | BJ1481 (ebook)

01/30/25

Unless otherwise indicated, Scripture quotations are from the New Revised Standard Version Bible, copyright 1989, Division of Christian Education of the National Council of the Churches of Christ in the United States of America. Used by permission. All rights reserved.

Scripture quotations marked KJV are from the King James or Authorized Version.

Scripture quotations marked MSG are from The Message. Copyright © 2002. Used by permission of NavPress Publishing Group.

Dedicated with deep love and joy to

The Brotherhood:
Andy Justice, Kwang Sik Chu, Matt Codling

TheoAdobo Collective:
Joyce del Rosario, Jay Catanus, Melissa Borja,
Rachel Bundag, Lisa Asedillo

The Quadrumvirate:
Mienda Uriarte, Bruce Reyes-Chow, Byron Wade

CREDO 69:
especially Kellen Smith

St. Augustine Fellowship of the Center for Pastor Theologians:
especially Todd Wilson and Gerald Hiestand

The Presa *Oikoumenē*:
Grace, Daniel, Andrew, Calvin (our puppy)

The Birth of Christ is the eucatastrophe of [humanity's] history. The Resurrection is the eucatastrophe of the story of the Incarnation. This story begins and ends in joy.

—J. R. R. Tolkien

Peace is joy at rest. Joy is peace on its feet.

—Anne Lamott

I have said these things to you so that my joy may be in you and that your joy may be complete.

—Jesus Christ

Kailanman ikaw lamang ang aking mahal
Kailanman ang tangi kong pinagdarasal
Minsan pa sana'y mayakap ka
Patutunayan na mahal kita

—Maso Diez

Translation from Tagalog:
You are always my only love
It's always the only thing I pray for
Sometimes I can hug you
I will prove that I love you

CONTENTS

Foreword by John D. Witvliet | ix
Acknowledgments | xiii
Introduction | xv

1 Joy's Truth | 1
2 Joy's Identity | 14
3 Joy's Speech | 30
4 Joy's Feast | 46
5 Joy's Work and Witness | 63

Epilogue | 79
Bibliography | 81

FOREWORD

In a world of biting political polarization, additive cell phone apps, catastrophic storms, and cruel warfare, a book on joy can feel entirely out of place. Thanks be to God that Neal Presa has defied convention to write one anyway. The book you are holding is a deeply personal countercultural manifesto—so countercultural that it may seem utterly surreal.

The very moment you and I begin to think, that may well be the transformational learning moment you and I most need—a moment that exposes the difference between the kind of fleeting happiness we often orient our spending of both time and money around and the kind of joy on offer from God through Jesus Christ in the power of the Holy Spirit. In my teaching I routinely attempt to invite students to discover the strong differences between merely ephemeral happiness and deep interior joy, shared in community. The more I teach it, the more I realize how much I need to relearn it, again and again.

So this is a book that invites us to set aside simplistic, shallow, and ultimately idolatrous desires for the kind of happiness on offer all around us, and to turn our attention to the deepest desires of our heart, the kinds of spiritual thirsts that are slaked only by the Holy Spirit of the living God.

This book is also an invitation to an entirely different way of going to church on Sunday.

Running through these pages is a conviction that Christian communal liturgical action matters because of the power of God, and a deep awareness of the most unusual way this power is unleashed through ordinary, messy, imperfect people, art forms, actions, symbols, and gestures—sometimes palpable and transparent, sometimes hidden and imperceptible.

At this cultural moment, it takes courage to claim that ordinary Christian worship services are a means by which the Lord is at work in our lives, restoring joy, hope, peace, and calm.

It is gutsy to imagine a world in which God is speaking and wooing us through others gathered in Jesus's name, uniting us to God and each other in bonds of fellowship.

It is a bold act of prophetic challenge to insist that liturgy challenges our pettiness and self-centeredness, our culture's penchant for commodification and cliché, our endless aimlessness and anxiety, hoarding and indifference.

Taking this book seriously challenges us to embrace an entirely new way of waking up on Sunday morning, an entirely new frame of mind as we get ready to walk or drive to a church service. That holds whether we are a preacher or musician or liturgist or dancer or deacon leading part of the service, or whether we have never been up front leading in our life and see ourselves more as a back-row kind of worshiper, eavesdropping on the proceedings.

For entering a church service with the same expectations that we bring with us into a theater or concert or lecture or arts festival or an evening of scrolling through YouTube will almost surely leave us disappointed. So much of the sustained value in it all simply can't be seen in real time. Some of it not only doesn't deliver on making us temporarily happy, it actually melts some of our temporary happiness away in service of a deeper joy. Sometimes it takes months or years for its sweetest fruit to ripen. And sometimes, our spiritual taste buds are not attuned to savor the kind of fruit it produces—the fruit of the Holy Spirit.

As I was led through the pedagogical liturgy of this book, my heart was drawn to the simple yet profound prayers at the end of each chapter. I encourage you to linger with them—and to pray at least one of them each time you get ready to walk or drive to church. Allow them to frame your own expectations and hopes. Take note of the phrases that ring true to you and also the ones that stretch you—the ones you need to pray aspirationally. Allow yourselves to be apprenticed by them. May we allow them to help us relinquish *both* our shallow sensibilities about the happiness we seek and typically too-thin liturgical theology we take with us to church on Sunday.

When we follow Dr. Presa's lead, and relinquish these smaller hopes for larger, deeper ones, we discover yet one more transformation—a healing of the rift so often experienced as we leave a church service and attend to demands of life in the world. Joy is not a fruit of the Spirit that grows only in church. And the healing offered to us in Jesus extends to the farthest reaches of all creation. The goodness of God is for nothing less than the "life of the world."

As I was reviewing this book, I came across Tim Soerens's exposition of the phrase *public joy*—an invitation to think of the ends of our economic life as instilling something more than more economic growth: "Public joy gets at the pulsing, hopeful, brimming-with-possibility kind of energy that by its very nature requires equity and justice, and celebrates both individual and collective agency."[1]

Ultimately, this book is about not only liturgical joy, but also public joy, creational joy, eschatological joy—joy as expansive as the loving embrace of the triune God. One of the apostle John's favorite refrains was the purpose clause "so that our joy may be complete" (John 15:11; 16:24; 1 John 1:4; 2 John 1:12). The vision here is of overflowing, abundant, extend-to-the-far-reaches-of-creation joy, joy that extends "far as the curse is found."[2]

The apostle wrote so compellingly "so that our joy may be complete." That only works if people read and wrestle with the apostle's inspired words. Neal Presa has been reading and wrestling and discovering the taste of that expansive joy, and he now invites us to do the same.

John D. Witvliet
Calvin Institute of Christian Worship,
Calvin University and Calvin Theological Seminary
Grand Rapids, Michigan

1. Soerens, "Subverting Two-Pocket Thinking," s.vv. "The Social Banker."
2. Watts, "Joy to the World," st. 3.

ACKNOWLEDGMENTS

Wrestling with God, reflecting upon the living God of love and the love of God was not a solitary matter, although there were many days that it felt like it. This season of taking a deep dive in recalibrating the heart and soul was done in community, and putting the thoughts in progress in book form engaged the listening ears, patient prayers, and loads of laughter from many.

My gratitude extends to Wipf and Stock, beginning with Michael Thomson, acquisitions and development editor, who through a digital meetup at Princeton Theological Seminary's online gathering sponsored by the Center for Asian American Ministry first heard my ruminations of this book. Thank you to managing editor Matt Wimer and his team for publishing this under the Cascade Books imprint, and to my friend/colleague and liturgical theologian par excellence John Witvliet, who accepted this as part of the Worship and Witness series. An extra thank you to George Callihan, editorial administrator, for graciously granting deadline extensions, and project editor Chris Spinks for shepherding this book to completion.

Even before I could prepare this book, there were eight years of heavy lifting as I needed to sort out and sort through what joy is, who joy is, and the tensions and challenges of life, faith, and ministry, not to mention COVID-19. In these eight years, I have been grateful to CREDO and my cohort number 69 that met October 31–November 6, 2017, at the Solomon Episcopal Conference Center in Loranger, Louisiana. It was there that I first began the rediscovery of joy. My deep gratitude to the Center for Pastor Theologians' St. Augustine Fellowship, which was and continues to be a community of thoughtful, insightful ecclesial theologians who take theology, worship, and the gospel seriously. Many thanks for the Louisville Institute, whose Pastoral Study Project Grant enabled our family to take a pilgrimage through Europe and for my eldest son, Daniel, and me to trek the monthlong Camino Santiago. Thanks to my pastor neighbor/

colleague Mike McClenahan for his support and guidance in preparation for the camino, and to Professor Kenda Creasy Dean at Princeton Theological Seminary for reflecting with me on this project and its implications. It was also the Louisville Institute that provided two Collaborative Inquiry Team grants that brought together two research teams focused on gender justice (for women in Asian American and Latinx churches) and racial justice (for Filipino Americans). These initiatives funded through the institute anchored this project on tangible efforts of transformative justice.

My heart overflows when I think of so many fellow sojourners on the Way, who traverse this liturgical pilgrimage. Most especially I think of my family: my wife, Grace; our sons, Daniel and Andrew; and even our four-legged family member, Calvin; our family hearth is where daily faith and love and joy are embodied and shared. I think of my ministry friends and colleagues who enrich my faith and who share the joys of serving the Lord and God's people, chief among them: Mienda Uriarte, Bruce Reyes-Chow, Byron Wade, Kellen Smith, Joyce del Rosario, Gabriel Jay Catanus, Melissa Borja, Rachel Bundag, and Lisa Asedillo. My best friends: Andy Justice, Kwang Sik Chu, and Matt Codling—they accept my humanity without judgment and love me to a fault.

With deep joy and love, I am blessed and give thanks to God.

INTRODUCTION

When I began ordained pastoral ministry in the Presbyterian Church (U.S.A.) in 2003, I came across a book that aptly described the rigors of the pastoral life: *Ministry Loves Company: A Survival Guide for Pastors*, by the late John Galloway Jr. This book was a healing balm in Gilead as I navigated the challenging early years of pastoral ministry. Not only did I begin a solo pastorate that year, but Grace and I, who had gotten married a year before, were also new parents. All in one year, I was learning how to be a husband, father, pastor, and homeowner, all while continuing my theological studies. John's book, and our friendship a few years later, was an encouragement because here was a veteran minister who named many of the tricky dynamics of ministry and life that I was experiencing and encountering in my first years of being a pastor, a newlywed, and a newly-minted dad.

In pastoral ministry since then, and, more broadly, in my marriage, parenting, and relationships, I have found so powerfully and personally that whenever faith and life are not nourished, joylessness creeps in. It enervates the soul, it tires the body, it runs down the mind. Nourishment in joy happens in the company of fellow sojourners. Faith and life are joyous and joy filled when done *in* and *with* company. But there's another aspect that I want to amplify in this book. Faith and life are joyous and joy filled when done *for* community. That is, when we engage faith and life in service for community, that's where joy sings. Because when we embody faith and life for the wider community of our common humanity, we see our greater purpose. When our faith and life desire and aim for the flourishing of all people, that there is justice. The Scriptures call this universal flourishing *shalom*. To strive for, work for, pray for the realization of that shalom is justice. And when our faith and life engage in that divine mission, joy is its fruit.

Life is pretty isolating and lonely as it is. Even with the seeming ubiquity of social media, there is much isolation and loneliness. We are more connected through technology, but those connections don't guarantee genuine relationships. When I was a youth, my pastor would say: "Tell me who your friends are, and I'll tell you who you are." I wondered back then if he considered that Jesus kept company with sinners. But there is a something to be said about my former pastor's adage: What company do we keep? Is the company we keep life nourishing and joy filled? Are the relationships in our lives inspiring us to work for universal shalom? Do we, likewise, inspire and encourage those in our relational orbit to live out faith and life for the sake and in service to the wider community?

It's no accident that the etymology for the word *companion* literally means "a fellow bread-eater." To have or to be companions, or to have company, means to accompany each other in eating. After all, so much of life and of work happens at table, with food, with drink, with conversation. Eating bread with each other is also about accompaniment on the journey, like a long hike through the forest or a long road trip, on a pilgrimage. You share food and stories with your companions. On the eighth day of our hiking the Camino de Santiago, Daniel and I arrived at the *albergue* (hostel) in Navarette, Spain. The owner of the *albergue* prepared a simple meal of pasta and salad and, of course, wine for the adults. There were ten of us gathered around a wooden table speaking English, Spanish, Italian, and French. We were intergenerational. In fact, there were three sets of fathers and sons, and one of them was a grandfather-son-grandson. Notwithstanding the linguistic barrier, there was a sense of community as we shared about our experience of the camino up to that point, what we looked forward to in the days ahead, and encouraged one another to continue on the journey.

When faith and life aren't nurtured and nourished continually and in community, bad things happen to the body, to the mind, and to the soul.

A few years ago, I came to a place in my life and ministry that was not good for the body, nor the mind, nor the heart. The pernicious thing was that it happened internally, outside the purview of my family and of my congregation. I managed to contain it so as not to adversely affect those around me, my loved ones, nor the congregation I served. I was faithfully producing what was both expected and desired from me—caring for people, loving them deeply, attending to meetings, being present at our family events and functions. But internally, there was a war waging. It was a battle of finding the essence of who I was, who I was called to be. I don't think it was a forties midlife crisis or grief over leaving a wonderful ministry in New Jersey and trying to get settled in a new ministry in California, with all the attendant sense of dislocation that occurred for my family and me. Nor was it that I went from being a solo pastor and the highest elected official in my denomination's governing body to taking a role as an associate pastor in Rancho Santa Fe, California.

Introduction xvii

I don't believe I was clinically depressed. I never got a diagnosis, but I didn't show any signs of depression. I slept well, I exercised regularly, ate a healthy diet, remained sociable. So what was this hidden sense that I was imploding inside, while outwardly I remained very productive and faithful in my roles of husband, father, pastor, son, brother, friend, and scholar?

On Ash Wednesday 2017, I was at a low point. Something was wrong, and I didn't understand it. Congregants in the evening service were invited to write down their troubles, sins, and brokenness on scraps of paper and toss them into a cauldron of fire to signify getting serious about ridding ourselves of sin and turning towards God. As I tossed in my scrap of paper, I covenanted with the Lord to do what the patriarch Jacob of the Old Testament did: I would wrestle with God. I needed to take this feeling of wrongness seriously. I needed God's help to change it.

Several days after that Ash Wednesday service, I stumbled upon the writing of King David in Psalm 51. This was a text I had read many times over the years, parts of which I had committed to memory. I had taught from this text on many occasions and led Bible studies on David's heartfelt prayer. There, in the middle of Psalm 51, were the words that leaped from the page:

> Do not cast me away from your presence, and do not take your holy spirit from me. Restore to me the joy of your salvation, and sustain in me a willing spirit. (vv. 11–12)

There it was, in plain print. The Word of God spoke to me, powerfully and personally.

It has been said that Psalm 51 was David's plaintive petition to the Lord after his adultery with Bathsheba and his arranging for the departure and consequent death of Uriah on the battlefield.

That's not the part of the text's context that I connected with. The thorn in my side wasn't adultery or murder.

What spoke to my weary heart and my parched soul was the joy of the Lord's salvation. In prior readings, I had often got stuck on the word "salvation." What did this mean for David? After all, David was the anointed monarch of God, called by God to serve the community of God's people. So, it couldn't be a matter of David's being "saved," whatever that meant. It couldn't be an issue of David wondering whether he belonged to God or whether God loved him still. Rather, David's prayer is about the joy of that salvation.

Like David, I needed the restoration of joy, the qualitative condition of what salvation's fruits are in my heart, the giving of a willing spirit. Psalm 51 makes clear what is required for that rejuvenation of life and faith: companionship. But not just any companionship. The text is specific. It is companionship with the Lord—the presence, the person, the promise, the power of the Lord. What King David experienced was lackluster solitude. It was an "as if" condition: as if the Lord had forsaken him, as if the Lord had pulled his spirit away, as if God's salvation was no longer with David. It echoed the fateful cry of Jesus Christ himself on the cross: "My God, my God, why have you forsaken Me?" (Matt 27:46, which repeats Ps 22:1). It is the felt human experience, deep down in the heart and soul of a person for whom joy has dissipated. It was my experience when the company I was keeping was no longer the companionship of the Lord himself, but only the surface-level appearance of the Lord. I had settled for the beautiful stained-glass windows in our sanctuary without the biblical stories being depicted in those windows. I was partaking of the bread and the cup at the Table for just the bread and the cup, and not so much as the communion of the body and blood of the Lord. In short, my parched soul could not discern and receive the life-giving soul of the God-given gifts around me. My heart and soul had been blockaded by the tasks, the functions, the expectations, the responsibilities, the obligations, the deadlines. I had settled for the stuff without the soul. I had settled for the frame and the colors and the canvas, but not really beheld the beauty of the painting, nor even the painter.

It felt as if the Lord had forsaken me.

These recent years have been pivotal and some of the most challenging of my life so far. It has taken a long while for me to arrive at a place where I can write this book. What the Lord propelled me to do as I wrestled with him was to see the glimpse of his hand through the gift of the liturgy: the liturgical calendar, the liturgical space of our sanctuary, the liturgical aesthetic of the worshipping community, and the wider liturgy of life. Liturgy, viewed comprehensively—not merely the text or the rubrics—is the gift that God provided me in this dark season. It was a hard reminder that the liturgy is God's gift to the church, the means by which the Lord enables his children to play in the sandbox of faith, hope, and love.

My scholarly discipline is as a liturgical theologian. The church's worship has a method, a rhythm, a movement. The church's worship through the ages apprentices us with patience as we await the promises of Advent to result in the birth of the Savior. The church's liturgy prepares us to reflect upon the Savior's servant heart in the shadow of the cross, all the while anticipating the victory of the Easter morning. What if we engage our life as liturgy? What if every part of our calendar were "liturgical," as it were? What would that mean?

The Louisville Institute grant that funded the Camino de Santiago pilgrimage was intended to be used in the summer of 2020, but the COVID-19 global pandemic forced those plans to shift to the summer of 2021. What first seemed like a delay was, in fact, a providential blessing. That yearlong period during the height of the COVID-19 pandemic was a sort of liturgical engagement. It was seeing in our circumstances the work that God was doing in, through, and among us. It was a hard time. It was a sacred time. We experienced the Camino de Santiago. We participated in protests for justice following George Floyd's murder. I engaged in research in an online community of scholars for Filipino American theologies. That period was an enriching period of liturgy in action because it was faith in action. It was faith ignited for worship of God for the sake of the community and in community. It was a period of deep joy.

My pilgrimage in, through, and with the liturgy was front and center at the onset of COVID-19. When shelter-in-place directives were issued for the state of California on March 16, 2020, I convened a daily morning prayer liturgy gathering on Facebook Live broadcast and Zoom that met from 5:30 AM to 6:00 AM Pacific Time every day, except during the summer months, until February 1, 2022. Family, friends, ministry colleagues, and strangers from all over the United States and around the world participated as we used the daily office in *Book of Common Worship: Daily Prayer* edition;[3] the Psalms, Epistle, and Gospel lections from the Revised Common Lectionary; occasional use of rites 1 and 2 of daily prayer from the Book of Common Prayer; and occasional use of "A Liturgy During a Pandemic" developed by Porter Taylor at the onset of COVID-19. The daily morning prayer liturgy gathering was a space for Scripture readings, then sharing of prayers of thanksgiving and prayers of intercession. Even after the scheduled time, people would post prayer requests or email me requests to share with the larger group. The early-morning period allowed those halfway around the world to participate before they slept, but I had also chosen that time in order to touch the lives of those in the United States who worked in the financial services industry, mindful that the New York Stock Exchange and the NASDAQ begin trading on weekdays at 9:30 AM Eastern Time. Because of the liturgical pilgrimage I had taken in the years leading up to COVID-19, I knew firsthand and had experienced how the triune God used the liturgy to recalibrate my life with joy; my prayer was that in some measure, the Spirit of Joy would impact the lives and choices of decision-makers who were navigating the uncharted waters of a global pandemic. It wasn't that I had joy, faith, and life all figured out; not at all. The struggle to get through COVID-19 was palpable. The loss of loved ones and colleagues who were sick in the hospital caused us to wonder how much longer we would shelter in place, or if our family would fall ill to the virus.

3. Presbyterian Church (U.S.A.), *Book of Common Worship: Daily Prayer*, 19–88.

Introduction

What I turned to in those online prayer gatherings was the church's liturgy. I found, as did the online community who joined me those mornings (evenings for those joining in Asia and the Pacific) was the prayers of God's people in the past and in the present. The church's liturgy focused on Scripture readings, particularly the Psalms. The Scriptures infused our struggle to be alive in the pandemic with a word from God about God. The daily liturgy we followed also included readings from the lectionary so we read texts from the Old Testament and the New Testament, including the Gospels and the Epistles. For me, the power of the lectionary readings connected us to the world of the Scriptures and with other worshipping communities around the world who were reading those same texts on that day. Our online gathering followed the daily prayer cues. Each day had particular prayers of thanksgiving and prayers of intercession for various human circumstances and geographical regions. For example, the prayer cues for Thursday included thanksgiving for "those who work for reconciliation" and intercession for "the church in the Pacific region." We concluded the intercessory prayers with the Lord's Prayer, which connected us to Jesus's own prayer and to every generation of God's people in every time and in every place who uttered that foundational prayer.

This book is about restoring and rediscovering joy through the spirituality of the church's liturgy. The liturgy is what life is really about. The liturgy expresses who we really and whose we really are. At the core of who we are is as child of God, created from the dust and to dust we shall return, as the "imposition of ashes" liturgy reminds us during Ash Wednesday. And liturgy is life, because every arena of our life—the so-called sacred and profane, the public and private aspects—is to be lived out as worship in the presence of God, who is our joy. In that worship, we are changed, we are transformed, and we are prepared to transform the world.

Throughout the book, I talk about the journey to restore joy in my life—joy in my pastoral vocation, marriage, parenting, friendship, faith, and all other areas of life—that began on Ash Wednesday in 2017 and that continues every day since then. While I will intersperse some experiences of my monthlong pilgrimage on the Camino de Santiago with our eldest son Daniel, this is not a recounting of that journey; you can read my Facebook posts of our daily journey from July 10, 2021, to August 8, 2021.

Even though I tell pieces of my story, this is not a personal memoir, nor is it a theological manifesto on joy. This book is about liturgical spirituality[4]—reflections on how worship, justice, and joy are all inextricably

---

4. Gleaning wisdom from the great liturgy scholar Louis Bouyer, Pfatteicher succinctly defines *spirituality* as "prayer plus love plus devotedness" or borrows from Brother Lawrence's description of spirituality as "the practice of the presence of God"

intertwined through the liturgy, and how all of these are expressions of the triune God.

The organization of this book follows the worship pattern of the five movements described in the 2015–2017 version of the Directory of Worship of *The Book of Order* of the Presbyterian Church (U.S.A.):

- Gathering Around the Word
- Proclaiming the Word
- Responding to the Word
- Sealing of the Word
- Bearing and Following the Word into the World[5]

These five actions envision the Lord's Day service when God's people gather in places of worship, summoned by the Word, expecting to receive the promise of God, congregating in community to pray, praise, confess, and be fed.[6] In communal worship, the triune God and the people encounter one another through Scripture reading, confessional prayer, liturgical dance, testimony of struggle and joy, sermon, baptism, the giving and receiving of the body and blood of Christ, intercessory prayer, prayer of thanksgiving, confessing the shared faith, stewarding and dedicating gifts for the work of ministry, and a benediction that deploys the people of God with the promise that the triune God accompanies them and meets them in the world.

These movements of corporate worship—in their parts and in their totality—parallel our pilgrimage through life. Each part and the whole experience are antidotes to those factors in life that stifle joy, that infuse our day with pernicious pettiness when compared to the injustices of the world, that obfuscate our holy responsibilities to love God, neighbor, and stranger. When the Spirit of God summons us to gather around the Word, this is a countervailing call over and against a tendency in the world to remain isolated or to gather around other words that cannot compare to the eternal Word made flesh in Jesus Christ. When the preacher proclaims a word from the Word of God for the people of God, she does so because the triune God has much to say about our lives, has much to interrogate about our choices

---

(Pfatteicher, *Liturgical Spirituality*, 10). More recently ecumenical leader Wes Granberg-Michaelson speaks of the interior and exterior dimensions of a liturgical spirituality as he cites late anthropological scholars Victor and Edith Turner: "Pilgrimage may be thought of as extroverted mysticism, just as mysticism is introverted pilgrimage" (Granberg-Michaelson, *Without Oars*, 91).

5. Office of the General Assembly, *Constitution 2015–2017*, W-3.3202, 104.

6. Pastor Paul Lang calls these elements of worship "maps of our atlas" (Lang, *Pilgrim's Compass*, 40).

and decisions, has much convicting and renovating work to do in our lives. Proclaiming the Word challenges our very assumptions and cultural impulses that place hope in other podiums—political, cultural, economic, or social. We respond to the Word through testimony, prayer, stewardship of offerings, engaging in the baptismal font, and partaking in the eucharistic feast. Through these responsive actions, the triune God inscribes and encodes upon our hearts the very life of the risen and ascended Christ, uniting us deeply in the heart and life of God.[7] The response to and the sealing of the Word recalibrates us to our core identity as children of God. When we forget who we are and live like orphans, we can wander through life aimlessly, joylessly, utterly lost. So the Word sends us, blessing us to be a blessing to others, to bear witness, to be "salt and light."

In other words, we gather at the beginning in order to be sent, to make a difference, to work for a better world, to love a bit more, to offer forgiveness in an unforgiving world, to feed the hungry even as we know others will remain hungry, to not cease clothing the naked and sheltering the houseless even as there are so many who will remain in those conditions afterward. This is the counterweight to the natural human impulse that instrumentalizes human relationships or will invest time and energy only if such investment can be monetized. When our days aren't regarded as lifelong liturgy, as worship done to the glory of God, then our going out and coming in on any given day become merely about the maintenance of our bodies, or pursuit of what culture tells us is "the good life."

These liturgical movements are elements, and each chapter is meant to be a standalone essay if you choose to read them in different order, but they are also sequential as they follow the worship pattern. I have come to appreciate and discover that the living Lord who is our joy will meet us and bless us whether we start at the "end" or at the "beginning" or somewhere in between. If you choose to start with the chapter on baptism, your entry point on the pilgrimage will be just as blessed as if you started with chapter 1. I'm a pastor, and I know well that there are church members who come forty-five minutes after the worship service started, arriving just in time for the Lord's Table. Or there are some who arrive only when the sanctuary doors are flung open, the benediction having been proclaimed, and the congregation is moving on to an afternoon church event involving food and a special guest speaker in the fellowship center. Are those persons blessed less than those who came early to reserve their pew? No.

---

7. For an example of a theology of joy that is shaped by the Trinitarian life and presence, see Everhard's explication of Jonathan Edwards's theology (Everhard, *Theology of Joy*).

Introduction

My son and I met some *peregrinos* (pilgrims) on the camino who chose to start at the Spanish town of Sarria, about one hundred kilometers from Santiago de Compostela, the minimum amount to receive the Compostela certificate of completion; we received the same Compostela even though we had hiked most of the eight hundred kilometers, starting from St Jean Pied de Port. Our Lord taught us a valuable lesson about receiving the same pay regardless of the time of day the laborers answered the invitation to work (Matt 20:1–16). I know how congregants will sometimes begin at the Lord's Table, coming to the eucharistic feast for many years, and then say, "Pastor, I have been coming here to the church for many years and I want to be baptized and confess that Jesus is Lord." While liturgically, ecumenically, and historically, the usual linear pattern of the pilgrimage is that you begin at the baptismal font and then go to the Table, just as with life, our pilgrimage is not so much a linear progression. Thus, your entry point to (re)discover the One who is our Joy comes at multiple points. Come with me on this brief pilgrimage. Our Joy beckons and awaits.

Soli Deo gloria.
Summer 2024

1

JOY'S TRUTH

> It is that of an unsatisfied desire which is itself more desirable than any other satisfaction. I call it Joy. . . . But then Joy is never in our power and pleasure often is.
>
> —C. S. Lewis[1]

Joy is elusive.

It's like happiness, but not quite.[2] It's like ecstasy, but it's not that either. Happiness is based on happenings. Joy is somewhat of the nature of Proust's memory of the madeleine cake, an unforgettable experience that you desire to be repeated but that cannot be strategized or manufactured for replication. It's not planned for; it's not scheduled in your calendar. You can't somehow tell Siri on your iPhone "Give me Joy" or set an appointment with Joy. With its sibling, Love, Joy grabs hold of you when you least expect it—and when it happens, you desire for it to happen again, and you want it to linger for as long as possible. Joy is about a vision for life, a commitment

---

1. Lewis, *Surprised by Joy*, 18.
2. Moschella opines on the wider and deeper dimensions of joy in contrast to happiness. She writes: "Joy also signifies a broader and more transcendent sense of goodness, one that links not just to personal well-being, but also to the larger reality, and to a vision of broader human flourishing. . . . It is linked to what we feel in our bodies and in our communities, our bodies of faith. Joy often arises out of deep interpersonal connections and the experiences of loving and being loved. It may also arise in communities of resistance to evil or injustice" ("Elements of Joy," 100–101).

of one's being, an alignment with our life's purpose. That chasm, that yearning, that desire for joy to be repeated comes from that human condition of being in the in between that the Lord's Prayer expresses in saying, "Thy will be done on earth as it is in heaven." It's as if the desire for Joy occupies the words "as it is in" between earth and heaven, because when we live life for what it is—the mediocre and sublime aspects, the ease and hardship—we seek an existence that is punctuated with glimpses of heaven touching earth, of earth cascading to heaven even for a moment. Joy is only momentarily experienced, but it has lasting effect. In his confrontation with God's work in his life, C. S. Lewis described it as "the same surprise and the same sense of incalculable importance . . . 'in another dimension.'"[3] What Lewis grappled with and what our lives long for is this tension of immanence and transcendence. It's a dilemma of the present tense and of that which extends beyond the present, all at the same time. It's as if the eternal realm is knocking at the fabric of the space-time continuum, and so what we experience as joy is the nudgings of eternity in our present context. It is heaven showing a bit on earth. To borrow C. S. Lewis again, joy is like the world of Narnia making a quick appearance on the other side of the wardrobe.

Fellow Presbyterian pastor Kathleen Bostrom and coauthor Peter Graystone suggest ninety-nine activities "to do between here and heaven" in order to enrich our lives and experience vitality. They include:

- Watch the sun rise
- Bake bread
- Read a Gospel in one sitting
- Give blood
- Examine an icon
- Give your testimony
- Plan your funeral[4]

Doing any of the ninety-nine on the list doesn't make you a queen or king of joy. These activities help in creating an environment where we think outside of our daily existence. But they are good starting points, nevertheless, in that they nudge us along on the journey to think outside of ourselves and to consider both the present tense with the future tense all in one swoop. Bostrom and Graystone's list is an example of immanence-transcendence.

---

3. Lewis, *Surprised by Joy*, 17.
4. Bostrom and Graystone, *99 Things to Do*.

These pages have taken seven years to pen. This book is deeply personal, not merely because of the personal and vocational struggle that catalyzed my pursuit of joy, its meaning, and its effect. It's also because of what writing about joy and the One who is our Joy means for my existence, and for the wider community to which I belong. To speak and write about Joy[5] is to attempt to capture experiences of toil, fervent prayer, ecstasy, hope, despair, love, hate—all with personal and communal implications. Joy is what happens when the Divine and humanity come together. In this deeper sense, it is to engage with the truth. How truer can one be when confronted with the voice and promptings in the heart of our Creator? How can I do justice to the subject matter? But the inward promptings of the Spirit give me the impetus and strength to write because the nature of Joy is like an uncontainable power and force that must be shared. I cannot hoard joy. That would be selfish and self-serving. Because it is the nature of Joy to be generous, to give, to love, I have a commitment and a delight to share what Joy has given me.[6]

When I have spoken about joy with neighbors and colleagues, and even strangers, they have all said, "Yes, we need more of that!" Because my writing began during the COVID-19 pandemic, the strains of and losses from COVID-19 forced us all to reexamine what life is about, especially when it comes to the role of work in our lives. Do we try to go back to what it was before, or do we step off the treadmill and pursue something else? I like how my longtime friend and colleague, Rodger Nishioka, put it, that this question is about the difference between "interruption" and "disruption." The former denotes an event that momentarily stops you in the track you're on, but when the event or circumstance passes, you continue on as you were before. Disruption, on the other hand, is an event or circumstance that stops you in your track, but when the matter passes, you move in a different way because you have been changed and transformed, either for better or for worse. Hopefully this period of great change and upheaval is of the disruptive kind. Joy is of that level and degree—we live differently because Joy encounters us. Of course, when Joy encounters us, we won't consistently live in the right way and make right choices that are life giving. But we become different in ways that are not immediately noticeable.

5. Because joy's source is the living God who is our Joy (like God is Love), I will sometimes capitalize the *j* to emphasize the living God but use lowercase for the experience of God's presence as joy.

6. Joy is meant to be shared. After narrating her riveting personal struggle and discovering joy in the process, Angela Williams Gorrell observed: "Joy, like other emotions, longs to be shared though. Expressing joy, as with other challenging emotions, requires support . . . we need permission to be joy-filled . . . we can organize spaces that are meant to invite and cultivate joy—spaces that suggest joy is both anticipated and welcomed" (*Gravity of Joy*, 173).

What is that something else that the disruptions of a global health pandemic caused all of us to reach for? The so-called #GreatResignation in the workforce of people leaving their jobs shifted to the #GreatReshuffle where people left their industries altogether to try other types of work. This then shifted to #QuietQuitting, where many are living in the silent mode of doing the bare minimum to earn their keep but are pining for something better.[7] The "something better" might be spending more time with their families or taking that longed-for vacation to Iceland. Perhaps it's going to a mission house build in Mexico, or simply being with friends and family who are life giving. COVID-19 pushed to the forefront a reassessment of what and who really matter in our lives. It forced us to a place of confronting our mortality and the fragility of life and human existence. It's a precarious place to be, daunting to engage life and death. Granted, life and death are something that billions of people on planet Earth are confronted with on a daily basis, faced with food and clean water subsistence or being victims of war and violence, sheltering from rocket fire, bombs, and missiles. For so many fellow human beings, it's not a matter of taking a vacation to reflect upon life, or of having the luxury of time and space to oneself; daily living is existing on the edge of the cliff where not finding a next meal or the act of stepping outside of one's home may mean the end of one's life.

Whether we came to the point of confronting our mortality during the pandemic or through some other experience, it's an important, if uncomfortable, exercise for all of us. No matter who we are, our days are fleeting, and we are engulfed in troubles to varying degrees and levels: "We are afflicted in every way, but not crushed; perplexed, but not driven to despair; persecuted, but not forsaken; struck down, but not destroyed" (2 Cor 4:8–9).

In every instance, when Joy is experienced, it involves more than me, myself, and I. Joy, by its quality, involves something else or someone else. Proust could not contain his joy of tasting and then recollecting the rapture of the madeleine cake. When we have experienced the love of neighbor, the love of God, the delight of being in the company of friends, we desire to share it. So we do so through writing, blogging, posting on social media, or simply describing it in conversation. Even testifying of a momentary joy with someone else increases the experience of joy when it is retold. I believe what the experience of joy needs is the divine vision or the divine agenda which the life of Christ embodied.

When we serve others—whether it be at a soup kitchen, or helping an older adult with their groceries, or paying forward the Starbucks coffee of the day for the customer standing in the queue behind you—we often

---

7. Klotz and Bolino, "When Quiet Quitting."

come away feeling good. Whether such a deed was done out of mixed motives—desiring personal recognition or needing community service hours to be accounted for—or out of purely altruistic impulses, the experience of momentary joy comes because you come to a realization that your existence is not isolated to your skin, your bones, your breath, your thoughts, your emotions. Life is not about you. And whenever we have the opportunity to give and receive from another, there's a qualitative texture that goes with engaging the other, of being connected to the other.[8]

We desire joy because we are created for joy. In my ecclesial tribe, one of the oft-quoted expressions of faith that summarizes who we are and what we are created to be comes from the seventeenth-century Westminster Shorter Catechism, which asks in its first Q&A the following: "What is the chief end of man?" To which the catechetical candidate responds: "To glorify God and to enjoy Him forever."[9] Our hearts long for something more when life becomes a slog through mundane daily tasks, because we are meant to live our days "to glorify God and to enjoy"—or, in other words, *find joy in*—"Him forever."

To glorify God and to enjoy our Creator forever is to live in the constant and consistent awareness of being in, dwelling in, abiding in the very heart and life of God. Notice how King David is "not afraid of ten thousands of people who have set themselves against me all around" (Ps 3:6) because "I lie down and sleep; I wake again, for the Lord sustains me" (Ps 3:5). Joy's wakefulness is not so much about eyes open to behold, but about being aware, basking in the presence of God. Yes, even in our sleep, when we are at rest, knowing, trusting, believing that we are cradled in the arms of God. Dearly beloved of God, trust in this testimony: "Likewise the Spirit helps us in our weakness, for we do not know how to pray as we ought, but that very Spirit intercedes with groanings too deep for words" (Rom 8:26). The profundity of that assurance that we are never far from the Lord's presence because even when we can't pray, such as when we are sleeping, or when we find it hard to pray, the Spirit knows us inside and out. The Holy Breath of God who is the Spirit of the ascended Christ, continues breathing life, consistently working, continues interceding, continues connecting us to the heart of God. The Spirit is our constant and consistent communication line, holding Jacob's proverbial ladder so that the Divine-human connection keeps flowing, never ending.

---

8. Pfatteicher reminds us that "worship is the admission of our creatureliness, the confession of our utter and complete dependence on God for life and being. It teaches us a selflessness that is unnatural to us, a generosity that we must learn to make our own" (*Liturgical Spirituality*, 13).

9. Office of the General Assembly, *Book of Confessions*, §7.001, 205.

As I shared in the introduction, I came to a place of lackluster exhaustion in my body, mind, and soul, and the Spirit of God knew what I needed at the right time. Outwardly, I was productive in ministry, in a new pastoral call, moved into a new home with great neighbors. I was in hog heaven in terms of productivity and efficiency. But my soul was parched, joyless. It was like the "walking dead," being aware of my surroundings, doing the work, performing the tasks, but not fully engaged, what can be described as "going through the motions." Joy had ceased being my companion, or the experience of Joy. I needed the Spirit to kick me in the ass, and that is what the Holy Spirit did by awakening me to the power of God's Word in a passage that I had read, taught, studied, memorized for decades since I became a follower of Christ and when I became ordained. Here it is:

> Do not cast me away from your presence,
> And do not take your holy spirit from me.
> Restore to me the joy of your salvation,
> and sustain in me a willing [or generous] spirit. (Ps 51:11–12)

There it was. King David's plea. Yes, the other sections of that chapter were equally important and caught my eye, "Create in me a clean heart, O God" and "Have mercy on me, O God" and all the rest. But it was those verses 11–12 and especially "Restore to me the joy of your salvation."

There I was gathered with God's people in that Tenebrae service in 2017 as we observed the promises of both Maundy Thursday and Good Friday in a contemplative worship service. At the pastoral invitation, each congregant and the pastors took a moment to reflect and pray and then, when ready, to take the slip of paper that was inserted in each worship bulletin and with pen or pencil in hand jot down words or phrases or a prayer where we confess or name those things that we desired to repent of in order to follow Jesus Christ more deeply and nearly. In all the times I did this exercise as both worship officiant, congregant pew sitter, or conference/retreat attendee, in this one time I had the hardest time jotting something down. Not that I wasn't aware of my sins, my pride, my brokenness; in fact, I couldn't write because I was aware of the few seconds we three pastors had, and at the appropriate time we three clergy would lead the congregation by lighting on fire our slips of paper using the paschal candle and then placing the fiery paper into a metal cauldron. This would symbolize that our confessed sins were being extinguished and we could begin anew a life committed to following Christ. The past-present was somehow forgotten, and we could face the future with confidence and certainty that our confession had been heard and received.

But I couldn't do it. Not because of lack of awareness of sin and my need of receiving again the promise of Christ. On the contrary. The slip of paper and the few seconds could not contain what was on my heart at that moment. The scripted moment did not do justice to what was happening in me, what I needed, what the Spirit must have been prompting me. I was paralyzed to write anything down because to write anything would mean to write nothing at all. To even put one word would not be what needed to be said. The Spirit came rushing into my heart with the words of God's Word, "Restore to me the joy of your salvation, and sustain in me a willing/generous spirit." "Do not cast me away from your presence, and do not take your holy spirit from me."

When I went through that period when I was stuck in a joyless rut, King David's words from Psalm 51 described exactly what I was feeling and experiencing: "Do not cast me away from your presence, and do not take your holy spirit from me. Restore to me the joy of your salvation, and sustain in me a willing spirit." It was as if the Spirit had left me, had vacated my soul, had left me bereft, had forgotten me. I was a living, breathing human being, married with two kids and a dog, an ordained Presbyterian pastor, with all my academic degrees, world travels, networks of friends and colleagues. There was much to be grateful for. But what I had missed or who I was missing was the Spirit of God.

The Spirit of God had not left me; it only felt that way, because I had missed what living and my human existence are really about. I had so focused on family, career, education, and serving—all good things in themselves, all noble callings, all part of who I am and what I'm called to be—but it was as if the Holy Spirit was merely among the priorities, when really what the living God desires, and I would dare say, demands, is preeminent place. It's not God, family, career, nor is it God, family, country. It's actually God *in* the family, God in the career, God in the education, God in the travel, God in the grocery shopping, God in the kids' sporting events, God in retirement. Joy is God's heart and life permeating every dimension of our life so we are changed to live oriented to God's presence.

The Holy Spirit awakened me to the reality that God restores the joy, God sustains the spirit, God's presence is constant, and it is I who walk away. It was I who was unmoored from my anchor, I who replaced God with those things that were good, but which I had turned upside down and understood as the highest goods in and of themselves. God helped me to see my foolish ways and set me on a path where he could "restore to me the joy of [his] salvation."

The Spirit of Joy enabled me to see that for King David, for me, for any child of God, it wasn't a matter of the loss of salvation, as if we can ever lose the love of God. God's love is steadfast. (Lam 3:22–23; see the constant refrain in Ps 136). God's love is unfailing and unending. Period. I trusted that then, and I trust it now. The prayer "restore to me the joy of your salvation" that the Holy Spirit impressed upon me is not a prayer pleading for some sort of entity called "joy" or some sort of magic amulet that we are given like a souvenir of our salvation. No! "Restore to me the joy of your salvation" is linked to "do not cast me away from your presence, and do not take your holy spirit from me," which is a plea. "I want you. I miss you. I desire you, Lord." It is a response to God's promise, "I am the Lord your God, and you are my people." In other words, Psalm 51:11–12 is a covenantal expression of love, of desiring to belong, wanting to be welcomed home again, to abide in the life and heart of God—and my plea was to stay there, because I had been adrift.

The first movement of worship—"Gathering Around the Word"—is the summons of the people of God to come from their homes, from their workplaces, to do something extraordinary. While God is present in those other places, there is something extraordinary in the specific place called "corporate worship" with the people of God ("And let us not neglect our meeting together" [Heb 10:25]). Think of the daily meals we prepare for ourselves and our families. Each meal is special. But there's something extraordinarily special when you plan a specific meal, with a nice tablecloth, with a roast that you would not regularly have, or the nice bottle of wine that was reserved for a special occasion, or that coconut cake that you purchased as a treat. Gathering around the Word with God's people is of that sublime character as it expresses an intentionality on the part of God's people to set aside a time and space to just "be"—be in the presence of God who will speak to us, who through God's people will inscribe upon our hearts a blessing. There is an expectation, anticipation, and hope that a word that will be said that will change us, that will let us know in a way that no other source can "I belong to God, and our lives have a bigger purpose than just maintaining our existence." Gathering around the Word reanchors us in a focused way that no other arena or activity can.

The 2015–2017 version of the Presbyterian Church (U.S.A.)'s *Book of Order* describes the purpose and elements of this first movement of worship, "Gathering Around the Word."[10] In this first movement, God's people are summoned to worship God through spoken words of Scripture and through songs that "proclaim who God is and what God has done." A prayer of confession names the power and presence of sin, and the efficacious reality of God's pardon, redemption, and claim upon our lives through Jesus Christ. In short, "the people give glory to God, and they may at this point

---

10. Office of the General Assembly, *Constitution 2015–2017*, W-3.3300, 104–5.

share signs of reconciliation and the peace of Christ." The gathering of the Word punctuates and disrupts our lives in order to recalibrate what we have done, what we have said, and what we have committed to do. In any given week or in any given day, we encounter many people, engage in meetings, and receive all sorts of information, not to mention what already lingers in our minds and hearts. The gathering of the Word calls us from the places we have been to intentionally be in the presence of God, where we can receive the truth of our lives and of this world. In the letter I wrote in 2020 as board chair to investors and friends of the Presbyterian Foundation, I reflected upon Ephesians 4:15–16, specifically that part of the epistle that exhorts us, "But speaking the truth in love, we must grow up in every way into him who is the head, into Christ." This is what I wrote:

> I love the word from Ephesians 4:15–16. It is a powerful reminder that each of us are knit together. That all of us are called to be part of the work of God, serving together to see that the whole body, the whole community flourishes to the glory of God. There's a powerful word and here's where I'll go Greek on you. That word "speaking" is not in the Greek New Testament of that passage. The ancient Greek term is a gerund (a verbal noun), so it should be "truthing," more accurately translated "But *truthing* the truth in love." This means that we have the gift and calling to have the truth of God, the truth of the Gospel, Jesus who is the Truth itself, in all that we do, in all that we say. In short, everything we do—even when we aren't speaking—bears witness to the powerful truth of who God is and who we are called to be.[11]

When we are gathering around the Word, the Spirit of the Lord is truthing us into the truth of God. The living Christ is Truth itself ("I am the way, the truth, the life" [John 14:6]), and the Spirit is acting upon us to shape us with, in, by, and into the living God so that we may embody and express who God is. Truthing the truth of God is less about dogma, doctrine, or a systematic theology; being truthed in the truth of God is living in the heart of God and expressing God's character, God's priorities, God's agenda, and God's justice for broken lives in a broken world. Whatever circumstance and condition we find our lives, our families, our churches, or our communities in, we need to be *truthed*. That is why I ended that same letter reminding us that we are "truthing the truth of God to do justice, love mercy, and to walk humbly with our God," repeating and underscoring the prophetic call in Micah 6:8.

11. Presa, "From the Board Chair"; emphasis in original.

My wife and I are empty nesters. Our eldest is a fourth-year college undergraduate; our youngest is a second-year college undergraduate. When I began this book, our youngest was still in high school. We each or together have been a Cub Scout den leader, Boy Scout camping leader, team parent for sports events, class parent, Dolphin Dad Day cheerleader, Career Days participant, and host to countless kids' birthday parties, including the famed LEGO-themed birthday party where my wife home-made LEGO-shaped cakes for eighty kids! Yet even with all activities, we as a family joined God's people for worship. Not just because I'm minister; even on vacations we would worship with God's people because of the extraordinary quality of doing so. We have been with many parents who wondered and pondered the value of church attendance and worshipping on Sundays even though they themselves self-identified as Christians, having been baptized in a distant time in a land faraway. These adults didn't care for church politics, or sometimes they had had a bad or awkward experience with a former church. And besides, they asserted, they could experience God at the beach, or at a sporting event, or at a friend's party get-together without all the drama of church and without the offering plate!

While it's true that we can encounter God in any place, there is something profoundly different about gathering around the Word in community to participate with intention in the scheduled, focused agenda of corporate worship. I love the beach. I find great peace communing with God in the presence of the sound of the seashore and in the beauty of a sunrise or sunset. When I go to the beach or when I hang out at a brunch with neighbors, yes, God is there. There is community to be found at a kid's birthday party or soccer game. But the purpose of those gatherings, and the focus of those places, is not God. So for me to go to those places to worship, I would have to purposefully detect God, to insert an intention that wasn't there and to reinterpret what is happening. The splashing of the beach surf in and of itself doesn't say, "God's love endures forever." I would have to read it into what's happening with the water splashing.

In the corporate worship of the people of God, let's be clear: mixed messages and misinterpretations happen all the time, too, and not everyone is on the same page. It's not that all the people gathered in corporate worship are all "holier than thou" and kind and generous and loving, or that all are listening intently to a sermon and agreeing on every point that the preacher intends. I know all too well that congregants are not on the same page, and it's human nature to have our minds wander.

But the stated goal and purpose of what's happening on that specified day and specified time—that holy date with God and with God's people, as it were—is to express our love and thanksgiving to God. We have a rendezvous to express to God our worries and anxieties, and hope that God will bless and strengthen us for life. We have this appointment with God, as with others gathered there, because life is hard and we can't go it alone and life last week or yesterday depleted me and I need a do-over and only God's promise of unending love can help my family and this world get to a better place. Whether every single person in that space is on board with that stated purpose 100 percent of the time is beside the point; the reason people will wake up at 7:00 AM and drive to the sanctuary is because they hope and expect that all those things will happen.

Even if everyone tries their best to focus and be in the moment as we gather around the Word, we expect that the rest of life will be on people's minds and hearts. We hope they'll bring that, too, because in that space we are human beings and we need God to know what we carry. How would it be possible to forget about the unpaid bill waiting at home, or the terminally ill family member lying in a hospital room, or the person we saw begging for food at the street corner on the way in? Lest we cease being human and forget the life we carry as we gather, we take all those things with us, because that is the expectation when we gather with God's people to worship the Lord. We are in the presence of the One who is our Joy, who restores the joy of our salvation, whose Spirit is not cast off, but who desires that we desire the Lord. God our Creator knows us more than we know ourselves. So when we appear inauthentic or all perfectly well in front of fellow parishioners, we aren't fooling God. God knows us inside and out. And so when we withhold our anxieties, our fears, and our shame, we are denying what it means to be fully human. How can we be in touch with the Living Joy who came to be among us when we withhold the essential part of being human: our brokenness and need of our Creator? And connected with that, when we present ourselves to fellow human beings as being perfect and unbroken, we create a barrier of distance from another who may see us as unwelcome to their plight. We may also be indicating our own inner desire to keep at arms' length the troubles of this world from the troubles of our heart. The result of this distancing is of humanity being inhuman and antihuman.

The desire for us to "Gather Around the Word" is that God-given desire and God's desire to see that joy is restored, that the Spirit is not cast off and that a willing/generous spirit is sustained in us. To gather around the Word in corporate worship is the antidote either to not gathering at all with anyone, living as if all that mattered was ourselves, or to gather around other words that are not for the purpose of glorifying God and enjoying God.

There's another challenge in "Gathering Around the Word" when we become unmoored from the One who is our Joy. Hanging around with others often has a specific goal with a beginning and an end point. You give the gift, you blow out the candle, you sing Happy Birthday. You follow the trail, you hike the woods, you take photos of the trees and birds, you return to your car. In corporate worship, "Gathering Around the Word" is not about being "done," although there is an Amen and a blessing to signify the end of the service. "Gathering Around the Word" is not and ought not be about efficiency, although sometimes it might feel like it when we try to script and control the time.

"Gathering Around the Word" says that Joy is not efficient, Joy cannot be contained and controlled. Joy is not a finished product or some end goal that we can expect when we punch in our timecard at 10:30 AM and clock out at 11:30 AM, as if the Spirit of Joy will meet us at the coffee cart afterward. The Spirit of Joy cannot be controlled nor strategized for. Remember Psalm 51:11–12: "Restore to me the joy of your salvation." God is the actor here; restoration occurs on God's terms, with God's work, through God's ways, at God's time. We can only ask. No pastor worth their position can guarantee that by 11:30 AM on Sunday that you will be fully restored with joy, that you will be on your way filled with hope and love and peace and all the spiritual fruit enumerated in Galatians 5:22–23.

What we can promise is that God will show up for you when you show up for God.

"Gathering Around the Word" is a call to Joy on Joy's terms. It is God who restores joy, it is God who effects joy. After all, to speak of joy is to speak of God's self as the One who is our Joy. The living God is not some entity that is acquired after we have blown out the candles or after the party is over and we are given a token souvenir to remember the occasion. The extraordinary quality of "Gathering Around the Word" with God's people for a date with God is that we are on the same page with our intent in going. The outcome may be different from person to person or week to week, but still the same God meets us and encounters us.

To know and believe and trust in that promise and reality is sufficient for our living out our days. To have that only—that God encounters us, that we are in the presence of God. To desire nothing else and no one else . . . not an entity called "peace," not a souvenir called "love," not a necklace called "joy," but the desire for the One who is our peace, the One is called "God is love," and to yearn for the One who is our Joy: that, beloved child of God, is the secret sauce to glorifying God and enjoying God forever.

FOR REFLECTION

1. What in your life makes joy a "fugitive" that is so elusive?

2. In what ways can you "Gather Around the Word" besides and beyond the formal worship service with God's people?

3. When was the last time you experienced the joy of God's salvation? What was it about that experience that was of an "infinite qualitative difference" rather than mere happiness?

PRAYER

Spirit of Joy, Lord of life, you make us worthy of your love through Jesus Christ our Savior. Restore the joy of your salvation by granting us generous and willing hearts, desiring you and your ways in every part of our lives. Abide with us and do not flee from us, even when sometimes we flee from you. Cling to us, and prod our attention so that when we walk wayward, your steadfast love tethers us to your heart, to your life, and to your way. Amen.

2

JOY'S IDENTITY

> For the secret of man's being is not only to live
> but to have something to live for.
>
> —Fyodor Dostoyevsky, *The Brothers Karamazov*[1]

In the opening line of the introduction to his bestseller *21 Lessons for the 21st Century*, Yuval Noah Harari opines: "In a world deluged by irrelevant information, clarity is power."[2] From birth to death for a modern North American, we are on information and data overload as to what we ought to be, what we ought to buy, where we ought to belong. There is a proliferation of apps that enable us and encourage us to access information at a whim. And we know all too well the ease of arranging for a same-day delivery through our Amazon Prime accounts. Digital media monetizes the volume of our usage, and banks on our drive to be connected. My teenage sons, from the time that they were in preschool, have known a world where the Kindle and the iPad had replaced lined paper as the primary means of communication.

My wife and I waited awhile, but the day came when we agreed to have our sons open up their own Instagram accounts. Our reluctance was due, in large part, to unknown strangers who may hijack their identities. But it was more than that. We wanted to wait until we believed our sons

---

1. Dostoyevsky, *Brothers Karamazov*, 320.
2. Harari, *21 Lessons*, xiii.

were emotionally, spiritually, relationally, and intellectually mature enough to navigate the many competing voices present in the digital space telling them who they are, or who they should want to be.

Our daily prayer has been that we would be able to form our sons in identities that were grounded in their being children of God and followers of Jesus Christ. Since learning we were expecting a child, my wife and I prayed daily for our child(ren) to become young men with a healthy sense of masculinity. When they each became Eagle Scouts, it was a pathway towards them being committed to serving the common good, students who excel with knowledge, athletes who exercise humble and confident sportsmanship towards their teammates and opponents alike.

What I found in wading through this season of parenting in the digital age was the touchstone of my own sense of navigating identity. For our sons, in addition to the usual pressures of being and becoming an adolescent and peer pressure, there was the challenge of figuring out two things in their words: owning the Christian faith as their own, being an Asian American, and being a young boy into becoming an adolescent and eventually a young adult. Because social media gives sound bites and is not a forum for in-depth analysis of the integration of one's faith with one's ethnic and gender identity, my wife and I provided open spaces for open, free dialogue with our sons about their Filipino, Korean American, Christian male identities. As well, we offered a generous posture for them to probe questions and doubts about the Christian faith beyond the doctrine and dogma of the Apostles' Creed that they memorized and learned as kindergartners. Because our sons grew up in largely White neighborhoods, we felt it important that they explore and engage their faith as Asian American male Christians. We had to continually be on the lookout for explicit and implicit messages and images of toxic masculinity, of racism, and of Christian language that was not generous towards others. So the deep challenge was navigating through the waters of ethnic, gender, and faith identities that were not siloed from each other but part of our sons' integrated selves. If anything, social media was another source of learning about wider culture and trends, but the crucible of formation of identity as Asian American Christian boys would occur in the arena of our family. It was in the context of our family conversations where we could sort through with them what they shared and struggled with in their peer interactions at school, in sports, at Scouts, at church, and in the context of social media where all their peers communicated.

Because I am part of the so-called sociological cohort called Generation X, I have been on this parallel journey with our sons of navigating my identity. When we don't attend to the soul work of who we are and why we were created by God, we become lost in the world. We are unmoored from what it means to be human, a beloved child of God. I have often been asked by colleagues why I do what I do. This is a shorthand way of asking, what is my "why." I say that I am committed to the hard work of ecumenism—of seeking unity in the Christian faith and in the broader human community—because of seeing the damage done to families and to the soul when churches divide as what happened to our congregation in 1995. I also lived in a home where every Sunday was contentious with my father wanting to go to the local Catholic parish and my mother wanting to go to our United Church of Christ (UCC) congregation. In the digital revolution, as my wife and I accompanied our sons in their navigation of identity, I, too, had to traverse that journey where global communication was happening through sound bites. To figure out what it means to be an Asian American Christian man who is a pastor theologian, husband, father, and all the various roles would require careful and prayerful analysis and reflection. Social media was helpful insofar as it quickly connected me to thoughtful influencers who combed the richness of the Christian faith and probing the margins. Social media provided snapshot summaries of blogged wisdom. But it was the face-to-face interactions over time, whether by many Zoom meetings or over meals, where the meaningful work of excavating identity towards integration happened. For example, one of the most life-giving friendships began as a professional connection with fellow Filipino American scholars at the American Academy of Religion. What began as a simple Google search on "Filipino American theology" resulted in a connection with the Rev. Dr. Gabriel "Jay" Catanus, who introduced me to Dr. Joyce Del Rosario. Then at the San Diego meeting of the American Academy of Religion at the Asian North American Religion, Culture, and Society Unit (ANARCS), I met Dr. Melissa Borja, Dr. Rachel Bundang, and Dr. Lisa Asedillo Pratt. At the present time, the six of us, together with many others with whom we connected through virtual conferences and gatherings, are working on a lifelong project on Filipino American theologies. This is all to say, social media helped to catalyze a connection, but the in-depth work happened in face-to-face community, augmented by virtual space.

As a pastor, I have found that the most prevalent concern of congregants is figuring out "Who am I? Who is God? What's the point of life?" I have had countless conversations with people who are either mid-career or in retirement and wondering what their work means or has meant. What does it all mean in the end, some of them wonder, to have invested three decades in a company, accumulating a stock portfolio and retirement savings? Or perhaps a divorcée wonders whether she can manage on her own, because her businessman ex-husband used to handle all the finances. A parent who stayed at home with their children as they grew might struggle with a sense of purpose once the nest is empty. These life circumstances bring to the forefront the question of identity.

A few years ago, I was invited to join a group of pastor alums from Princeton Theological Seminary for a sponsored pilgrimage to the Holy Land. Our group was led by Princeton's noted New Testament archaeologist professor James Charlesworth, who also was director of the Dead Sea Scrolls Project. Charlesworth had encyclopedic knowledge of every sacred site and the latest archaeological digs. We traversed an area around Caesarea Philippi, where Jesus had asked his disciples the pivotal question on identity, "Who do people say that the Son of Man is?" And then he had asked the more pointed question, "But who do you say that I am?" (Matt 16:13b, 15b; also Mark 8:27, 29). As we stood in the vicinity where Jesus most likely had asked that question, Charlesworth pointed across the Tiberias and explained that there was likely a superstructure in view, that the sun shining upon the white limestone would have refracted a shimmering edifice for the whole region, a temple dedicated to Emperor Caesar Augustus. It became clear to us that in saying this, Charlesworth was impressing upon our imaginations the urgency and gravity of Jesus's query to the disciples. In light of the vision, mission, and values of Caesar and all those who pledge their allegiance to him, who do you say that I am?

In my pilgrimage of seeking the restoration of joy, I was confronted with those central questions of identity that so many in my congregation have asked me. "Who am I to Jesus? Who is he to me?" I am an accomplished pastor theologian with a loving family. I've traveled widely and seen so much of the world. But who am I? Who is he to me? Am I following the vision, mission, and values of Jesus Christ? Deep down, have I been about the success of my own vocation, my own sense of accomplishment in serving the church, the academy, ecclesial councils, books and publications, my family, and the communities I have lived in and loved? Has my life been about those things, those people, those degrees, those milestones?

Has my sense of identity been rooted in Jesus or in the way others see me?

Those were the deep-rooted questions I was confronted with and which the Lord helped clarify for me. When your identity has been hijacked by others telling you who you are, or you convincing yourself of who you are, then you'll find yourself in deep trouble.

When I was a solo pastor in New Jersey, the elders and I made a slight liturgical innovation: we moved the portable baptismal font to the middle of the aisle. We did this to put in plain view the so-called tomb and womb of the faith: we die with Christ in the water; we are reborn in Christ from the water. One charter member of the church who found the new placement inconvenient and annoying remarked one Sunday, "That font is in the way." And that was exactly the point: the baptismal font is in the way. The font disrupts us because we have to continually deal with what is being declared and promised by the Lord through the font—the water, the liturgy, the prayer, the pronouncement. There at the font the Lord disrupts us to consider what it means to be a fragile human being who lives every second by the mercy and grace of God. Imagine, when someone who is a Christian dies, the Christian faith says that the deceased have completed their baptisms. On Ash Wednesday, as the sign of the cross is placed on people's foreheads with grey or black ash, the pastor says: "Remember your baptism and be thankful. In the name of the Father, and of the Son, and of the Holy Spirit. Amen." The font is one way where the Spirit of the Lord prompts us to consider God's work in our lives and that we belong to God no matter where we are, what we do or don't do, what we hope for and what we are scared to hope for. The font declares God is for me even before I have knowledge of God or even before I acknowledge God. The Lord has called me God's beloved child because of the Lord Christ. That identity, inscribed by water and sealed by the Holy Spirit, indelibly marks who we are and what we are about. Instead of regarding baptism as something "one and done" in a time and place far away, let us regard baptism as the spring from which our identity as child of God continually is recalibrated. The Lord's promise at baptism is a ubiquitous declaration if we will remember and pay attention to what baptism is about as the foundation—the fount—of our faith. Baptism is about identity. Baptism is a clear affirmation in words, in the experience of splashing or sprinkled water, and in the context of the gathered community where God is saying to us: "No matter where you go, what you do, or what the culture says you are to be and become, you are my child and I am your God." Joy's identity, therefore, springs from baptism because the living God is speaking and acting through the baptismal waters.

Serving in sunny Southern California and being near the beaches of San Diego County allow me the privilege of doing beach baptisms. I've done several baptisms for confirmation students and even one for a seventy-year-old member of our church. The most profound experiences have been the beach baptisms of toddlers and adolescents in the past few years. One by one, I led them to the incoming and receding waters as the grit of sand ebbed and flowed between our toes. Trying to keep balance in the rushing water while the sun blazed above, the white foam of the Pacific waters splashing around us, I declared, "I baptize you, in the name of the Father, and of the Son, and of the Holy Spirit. Amen!" I have thought of those moments in prayer, wondering when in the years ahead the child will encounter both the joys and the deep struggles of life, in what poets have called the "Land of Unlikeness."

The power of baptism and the visible reminder of the baptismal font are in declaring, and then, through visible engagement and reflection, restoring our identities rooted in joy. Baptism's promise is that when our identities are easily and consistently hijacked by forces within us and external to us, we are brought back to our compass. At its core, baptism calibrates our existence as daughters and sons of God.

We have to address the conundrum of baptism. The dilemma with baptism and the divine promises in baptism is that we as human beings remain in a vulnerable and fragile condition. One would think that if God is for us, who can be against us. If I know in the deep recesses of my being that I am a child of God, then I should be okay. If it's a matter of acknowledging, trusting, and knowing all those truths, then I should be okay. The assumption is that joy will be our constant companion if I can continually affirm the truth of baptism and what baptism means. But that's not the case. Baptism is not some magic pill by which, once taken, we will never experience melancholia, sadness, or joylessness again. On the contrary, joylessness is a constant companion on the journey. That is why I am writing this book and have spent considerable time in prayer, reflection, reading, and writing on this subject for all these years. The promise of baptism's joy lingers with us for a lifetime, just as the promise of joylessness also holds us by the hand as we walk the journey. That is why we need the church's liturgy. Baptism holds joy and joylessness in healthy tension. Baptism is a matter of mortification and vivification: a matter of death and of life. In descending into the baptismal water (whether by plunging, being dunked, being splashed, or even receiving asperges), we are sacramentally entering the tomb with Christ, dying with Christ. Our hearts are being mortified with him. In our ascending from the water, we are sacramentally rising with Christ at his resurrection. The baptismal water is both tomb and womb—dying with Christ and being rebirthed with Christ in newness of life. It's this constant, dyadic tension that accompanies us our whole life: life-death, joy-joylessness, cross-resurrection.

Being a child of God and being reminded again and again of that core identity has influenced who I am and how I live. Holding that identity in my heart shapes my motivations for what I do. I have found when that core identity is hijacked by others' expectations or by what I think my vocation should be about, then joy quickly dissipates. A lackluster spirit sets in and dries up joy, because it's like I have begun to live again as a spiritual orphan. If I don't live as a child of God, then I am lost. Note that it's not being childish; it's being childlike.

Living as a child of God is to know our limits. Living as a child of God is to know in every part of our being that we are always dependent upon the Lord for what we have and what we ever will have, who we are and who we will ever become. This also means that we deeply trust in the favor and goodness of God as our heavenly Father, whose love is like that of a mother who nurtures us, who is our protector, our refuge, and our strength, who has our back. Always. A child who knows deep down that their parent is both able and willing to move mountains is free to generously love, to dance in the streets, to sing for joy, to dream big dreams, and to pursue those dreams. A child who knows deep down that their parent has their back always knows that when he or she makes a mistake, the love of the parent will come rushing out to embrace them on their way back home.

When I was seven years old and in the second grade, my teacher, Mrs. Genie Ramstetter called our home. This was early evening, and it was unexpected. Mrs. Ramstetter spoke with my mom and said that since I was excelling in every subject, she had proposed to the school principal that I skip the third grade. When my parents asked if this was what I wanted, I leaped for joy and said, "Yes! Yes! I'm going to the fourth grade! I'm going to the fourth grade!"

It wasn't until after the meeting with the principal the next day to finalize plans that nervousness set in. I had seen the fourth graders at lunch and at recess. They were tall. They were athletic. Did I say they were tall? They were.

As we were driving home, my mom said she was proud of me. She recounted to me how I was born two months premature. I had heard this story before, but my mom wanted to tell it again with emphasis. She said I had weighed four pounds, if not less. My body's length was the length of my dad's forearm. I couldn't breathe on my own, and the doctors hadn't known if I was going to make it out of the hospital. I was kept in an incubator for several days. As my parents looked through a book of babies' names, they stumbled upon "Neil," which means "champion." My mom was intentional about choosing that as my name because she wanted her firstborn child to be a champion in everything. She wanted me to succeed. She prayed that I would succeed out of the incubator. She prayed that I would succeed in life in the next few days and, beyond that, in the life that was in store. She also chose the less common spelling for my name: *n-e-a-l*. She said that I was special, and I should have a special name with a distinctive spelling. To complete my name, they took my dad's name Noel and reversed it: *l-e-o-n*. They wanted to instill in me that I am my father's son. So when I got baptized, I was baptized Neal Leon.

My mom told me that story in the car ride. She was reinforcing my identity as I faced a new challenge as well as reminding me that she was there to have my back.

She told me the same story a few years later in the car ride home after I learned that I had successfully gained entrance to Lowell High School in San Francisco, one of the finest public high schools in the nation. Again, I had worked hard to achieve something, but when faced with the reality, I felt nervous. Again, my mom told the story of my birth name. She told me I was a champion, and then she said, "I will do anything for you. I love you."

I remember both of those events like they were yesterday. They are vivid memories of joy. Not because the outcome was that I skipped the third grade or that I got to go to Lowell, although those were good outcomes. I remember those events because Mom's love knew no limits, and the joy that I felt was anchored to Mom reminding me of whose I am, who I am, and the hopes and dreams instilled in me.

So when I had the crucible journey a few years ago that gave rise to this book, it was a journey to rediscover that core identity. My pilgrimage of joy was a painful one because the Lord helped me to peel away the identities I had used to replace that core. It's not that I stopped being a pastor, a husband, a father, a son, a brother, a friend as I rediscovered my core identity. It's that I had served in those roles and in those callings separated from what it meant to be a child of God, and I needed to reintegrate my baptized identity into the whole of my life. I had instrumentalized faith and become duty bound to the task of pastoring, to the task of being married, to the task of being a father. Those roles seemed to become unhinged from the baptismal calling of being child of God. To be faithful, the Lord helped me to see that I am a child of God who is a husband/father/pastor/son/brother/friend. What informs how I am in those roles is the foundational vocation of being a child of God.

Why does this matter? Because if we don't see our roles and callings through the lens of being a child of God, then when we falter, we think or we are told that we have mortally failed as a spouse/parent/(fill in your job)/daughter/son/friend. Or, on the flip side, if we are successful in those areas, we might be tempted to think we owe our success to our own ingenuity, rather than to the Lord who has blessed us with skills and gifts. Keeping at heart our core identity as a child of God keeps at bay sinful pride. Being a child of God frees us to accept our failures, knowing that we are forgiven and redeemed and called to make right the wrong. Being a child of God also frees us to direct our hearts to give credit where it is due when the way we live has been praiseworthy.

When our eldest son, Daniel, and I hiked the Camino de Santiago the summer before he would start college, we ventured off on the month-long adventure through rough terrain and quiet vistas of fields of wheat and sunflowers. It was a pilgrimage of honest relating one to another. We shared laughter over surviving two near misses of being mowed down by a wheat farmer's truck. We had frustrating arguments over my failure to keep pace with my youthful companion. There was a moment that I captured with my phone camera when Daniel went about five minutes ahead of me on a meandering road that seemed to go on forever. With fields on both sides of our clear line of sight, it was just him and me on that lonely road, with the blue sky above. It was quiet, the wind gusting only slightly, and I could see his backpack bouncing up and down as he walked. He was going farther and faster, and I was hanging back, teary eyed, saying a prayer. I prayed: "Heavenly Father, you knew Daniel when he was in Grace's womb. You knew him from the very beginning. You have watched him. You have been with him. Carry him to the adventures that await. You have him, Lord. Protect him. Meet him wherever he will go, because I know you are there for him. Thank you for loving him, and thank you for giving me the opportunity to be his dad. Protect him, Lord. I let him go into your hands. I trust you, heavenly Father."

That was my prayer at that moment. I framed that photo and placed it in his college dorm room with the first Bible verse I memorized when I came to faith as a high school student. It was one of the first Bible verses Daniel and Andrew learned in Sunday school: "Trust in the Lord with all your heart and lean not on your own understanding. In all your ways, acknowledge Him and He will direct your path" (Prov 3:5–6 KJV).

As I uttered that prayer on the camino, my memory went to the day Daniel was baptized as an infant. I recall my pastor colleague, Rev. Joseph Yoon, who baptized Daniel, had prayed, "Be with Daniel wherever he goes." Grace and I reflected upon that moment the following day, reflecting that wherever Daniel goes, whatever he becomes, God's love for him is foolproof. We had to put our faith to its utmost: What if he grew up to be a convicted criminal, a terrorist? Can we say that God is with him, too, loves him still? And we say yes because baptism says, "Yes, I am for you. Yes, I am with you. Yes, I will never let you go. Yes, I got you."

That's a radical truth and reality of baptism, and that is the freedom that is embedded (or en-fonted) in baptism. God in Jesus Christ is for us. Full stop.

The Lord did additional work of renovation and refurbishment in my life during this season of reflection. The promise of the gift of baptism, what the late liturgical scholar Laurence Stookey called "Christ's Act in the

Church,"[3] is not merely about my identity as child of God, as though it were somehow focused on my isolated existence, my personal salvation, my own belonging to the triune God. No—baptism, like every gift of God for the people of God, is a seal of Joy. It is about the flourishing of the entirety of creation and every creature that "dwell therein" (Ps 24:1 KJV). It is about the justice of God and the God of justice, because justice is God righting the wrongs, the Lord bringing about shalom transformation so all of creation is made new. Baptism, then, is not distilled to just my well-being, nor even just about my kin in the *kin*-dom of God. Nor is it just about my congregation, nor limited to my ecclesial tribe. It is about the flourishing of all.

The Spirit of life awakened me to this truth when I began teaching at Union Theological Seminary in Dasmariñas, Cavite, in the Philippines, about an hour drive from the home of my paternal grandparents. I teach in person and online for the seminary, which has been dubbed "School of the Prophets." This school has historically been about advocating for the marginalized, being in solidarity with the oppressed, and equipping and supporting activists who have been on the front line. Their alumni/ae are minister-scholar-activists who have spoken truth against the martial law imposed by former Philippine President Ferdinand Marcos, holding accountable succeeding presidential administrations. More recently, alumni/ae have protested against former President Rodrigo Duterte and current President Ferdinand Marcos Jr., both of whose human rights abuses are well documented by human rights organizations and the United Nations Commission on Human Rights.

Here were my students—all pastors, all ministry practitioners—putting their lives on the line for the sake of justice, fighting for my parentland, their land, their livelihood, their ministry; for them, justice was not an extracurricular activity or one program priority among several. Justice was the very essence of the faith. To confess and to live out the belief that Jesus is Lord meant to work, to struggle, to pray that God would right the wrongs of political corruption, systems that maintain the wide disparity between the haves and have-nots, and a judicial system beholden to political and economic elites. Here I was as a Filipino American Pacific Islander, a child and grandchild of the Filipinx diaspora, across the ocean, across the water.

It is water that connects land masses around the world, and it is in the water, swirling in the Pacific, where the so-called Great Pacific Garbage Patch floats, measuring a walloping 1.6 million square kilometers (twice the size of Texas's land mass). The Pacific Ocean has also been the site of war game maneuvers between the United States and China as each side flexes and tries to assert their respective military and economic hegemony.

3. Stookey, *Baptism*.

As baptism is the seal of the One who is our Joy, it is the declaration of God's claim on everything and everyone. This means, then, that there is an expansive, cosmological significance and consequence of baptism. Baptism is comprehensive in its embrace of the triune God's benediction upon the entirety of creation: "It is good." This also means, then, that all those who are baptized, and the ecclesial communities to which they belong, are saved and loved for the purpose of being initiated into the justice-seeking work of the Lord. That is, to live a salutary baptismal life is to do so in service to the God of justice. It is to belong to the One who desires for all to be fed, to be clothed, to be set free from the powers and principalities of sin and from all that seek to contradict or contravene the joy of God and the God who is our Joy.[4]

Reformed theological traditions, specifically my own ecclesial tradition, the Presbyterian Church (U.S.A.), have a robust understanding of what baptism is about and what goes on at baptism. Here are some of the key descriptors of the richness of this sacrament:

- The sign and seal of our incorporation into Jesus Christ
- Dying and rising with Jesus Christ
- Pardon, cleansing, and renewal
- The gift of the Holy Spirit
- Incorporation into the body of Christ
- A sign of the realm of God
- A sign of God's covenant
- Linked with the waters of creation, the flood, and the exodus

---

4. I am grateful to my ecumenical colleague and friend, Ruling Elder Dr. Dianna Wright, director of Ecumenical and Interreligious Relations for the Presbyterian Church (U.S.A.), who during a conversation at the Eleventh Assembly of the World Council of Churches in Karlsruhe, Germany (August 31–September 8, 2022), discussed with me the WCC's Pilgrimage for Justice and Peace. She correctly noted that for many, the terms "pilgrimage" and "pilgrim" are traumatic, particularly Indigenous peoples in the United States, for those terms mean European settlers in the seventeenth century who ravaged Indigenous communities in the so-called New World. Thus, Columbus Day in the United States is renamed Indigenous Peoples' Day. The conversation brought me to thinking about the terms, as has been the aim of this book and the assertion I am making, that to live and walk a "pilgrimage" must be shaped, informed, propelled by God's transformative justice, which is an act of worship, which is the joy of the Lord's salvation. When we disjoin that triad for the other dimensions, injustice, violence, despair, and the hegemony of the self overtakes, as human history is sadly replete with examples.

- Connects us with God's creative purpose, cleansing power, and redemptive promise from generation to generation
- A sign of God's gracious covenant with Israel
- A sign of God's gracious covenant with the Church
- Represents God's call to justice and righteousness, rolling down like a mighty stream, and the river of the water of life that flows from God's throne
- Enacts and seals what the Word proclaims: God's redeeming grace offered to all people.
- At once God's gift of grace, God's means of grace, and God's call to respond to that grace
- [As a means through which] Jesus Christ calls us to repentance, faithfulness, and discipleship
- [As a means through which] the Holy spirit gives the Church its identity and commissions the Church for service in the world
- The bond of unity in Jesus Christ.
- [Through baptism,] we are made one with Christ with one another and with the Church of every time and place.
- Witnesses to the truth that God's gift of grace calls for our grateful response
- Marks the beginning of new life in Christ[5]

The Reformed theological traditions affirm and recognize the centrality and foundational nature and character of baptism in that other "pastoral and occasional services are all rooted in the baptismal covenant and flow from the promises of Baptism."[6] These include services involving the reaffirmation of the baptismal covenant, welcoming God's people to the eucharistic Table, welcoming new members, commissioning for mission service, ordination and installation, memorials and funerals, censure and restoration, and marriage.[7] The depth of baptism's efficacy includes and projects beyond any one individual and any person's identity. The public nature of baptism orientates us to our identity in relationship to the whole.

A few years ago, my best friend and I set out to articulate a statement of our vision, mission, and values as men of God, disciples of Jesus Christ,

---

5. Office of the General Assembly, *Constitution 2019–2023*, W-3.0402, 92–93.
6. Office of the General Assembly, *Constitution 2019–2023*, W-4.01, 101.
7. Office of the General Assembly, *Constitution 2019–2023*, W-4.02–4.07, 101–7.

brothers in the faith, husbands, and fathers. He is a robotics automation sales engineer who works with business development matters in his company. So when I mentioned mission, vision, and values for our lives and our vocation, he knew immediately what I meant. After all, any company that doesn't have a clear (and compelling) vision, mission, and values will not be managed well. Employees won't have a clear sense of purpose, customers will wonder what this organization stands for, and investors may question the prospects of future growth without direction. So Andy and I set out to discuss what we valued, and we aggregated our years of reflecting upon faith and family and work into one succinct statement. At its core, the statement is an identity based on baptism. The statement's frame is being children of God through the various roles and functions we have in our respective fields, in our homes, and in the community. It's a statement that helped me in this pilgrimage of joy.

HEEDING CHRIST'S VOCATIONAL CALL UPON OUR LIVES

Andy Justice and Neal D. Presa

VISION STATEMENT: Committing every facet of our lives (work, family, recreation), relationships, and decision-making to the double commandments: to love God with all of our heart, soul, mind, and strength; and to love our neighbor as Christ loves us.

MISSION STATEMENT: To strive for excellence in our respective fields with godly integrity, bringing our Christian faith to bear on our word and work in public arenas, serving the common good to transform the world to God's glory, and dignifying the intrinsic value of all people as those created in the image of God.

We value:

- People—colleagues, superiors, subordinates—as all people are gifts from God, whose gifts and experiences enrich our own, who challenge us to grow, who are bearers of the divine image and therefore are not to be commodified nor exploited.
- Family—being faithful in our marital vows, nurturing our children in the Lord's ways, providing spiritual leadership, and giving of ourselves to them through time, presence, love, empathy . . . all by God's grace.

- Grace—because we continually fall short of others' (culture, our professions, society, family, church, etc.) and even our own expectations of ourselves, we place our trust and confidence in the God who through Jesus Christ by the Holy Spirit already and fully accepts us, that there is nothing we can ever do or not do to diminish or increase God's sure love for us. We are and forever are forgiven.

- Sabbath—this means not only and merely Sunday as the holy day to gather with our church community and family for worship and Christian education, but we value regular rest, periods of reflection, recreation.

- Prayer—not only and merely as a means to offer ourselves to our heavenly Father who promises to hear our petitions, but also through prayer God speaks to our hearts, shaping and forming us. Prayer expresses our constant need of God's guidance and direction.

- Purity—purity in our actions, purity in our thoughts, purity in our decision-making.

- Stewardship—we are stewards of all that God entrusts to our care—management of people, resources, organizations. We don't own things; we are not lords. We take seriously our responsibility. "To whom much is given, much is expected." As we excel in our respective fields and are placed in positions of increasing trust with broader jurisdictions, we seek to be servant leaders.

This mission-vision-values statement that Andy and I crafted many years ago still informs and shapes who we are and whose we are and why we do what we do in the various arenas to which we have been called. Once a year when we celebrate our birthdays or when we have our annual hangout to catch some tennis at the BNP Paribas tournament at Indian Wells, California, we invariably mention this in some way as a reminder. We do an annual check-in so that our shared mission doesn't get lost in the avalanche of work emails, deadlines, family responsibilities, and cultural messages that are not always salutary to the soul.

One of the things I so appreciate about my brotherhood and friendship with Andy is its authenticity and truthfulness. We take God seriously, we take ourselves seriously (though not too seriously!), we take our sins seriously, and we take God's grace seriously. What this has meant is real conversations that are not judgmental—naming our brokenness, oftentimes exchanging expletives because of pet peeves or abhorrent things that make life less joyous. Ours is not a sanitized, sit-still-in-the-pews, keep-quiet, fold-your-hands, and look-holy sort of friendship. Our more than two decades of deep friendship are powered by the sacred bond of discovering and embracing what it means to be human. We continually acknowledge that as baptized children, as adult men, we are in need of abundant grace, because we don't have life figured out. We don't have ourselves figured out. We may be working professionals, but we are very much God's handiwork, which is still being reconstructed and reconfigured.

Andy will tell you that when we get together, the beach is where I recalibrate best. Perhaps it's because I'm a guy of the Pacific, having been born in Guam. But there have been many times when he and I will just sit, watch the sunset, and be in the moment. We hear birds overhead and see little crabs scurrying about. We notice a sandpiper making tracks in the sand and a distant sailboat or a surfer trying to catch a wave. The sight of the water, the smell of the ocean, the sound of the tide's ebb and flow, the light that shimmers from the sea's surface, the quiet breeze that caresses and whispers—all of this is life giving.

I think what Andy and I did was reconfigure and reorder for ourselves the way society understands life's priorities. It's been said in the investment and financial planning world that we spend one third of our lives learning, one third of our lives earning, and one third of our lives returning. Think of the seasons of life and of parenting. There's a great deal of time spent in the first third trying to learn how to ride a bike and swim and position oneself to get to the right college. Once in college, you try to figure out the right major and the right internship to land the right job. And when you land the right job, it will probably be the right job only for a season, and you may have ten more jobs along the way. Perhaps there will be two or three career changes thrown in the mix. And then you hope and pray that you have squirreled away just enough to retire so that you can enjoy your pension, offer some volunteer hours, and raise grandchildren or mentor the next generation. Learning, earning, and returning. And when you ask what people's priorities are in that learning-earning-returning, most people will say: family, friends, God, work, health, or some variation on that theme.

But what Andy and I came up with changes that. *Baptism* changes it. It's not a priority list of family-friends-God-work-health or God first, then family, then family, then work. Rather, it's God infiltrating and permeating every arena, every part. So that your mission, vision, values is God *in* your family, God *in* your friendships, God *in* your work. Or to put it in the three-point schema: God in our learning, God in our earning, God in our returning.

The Spirit of Joy, the One who is Joy, gives us our identity from our birth—and when along the pilgrimage of life we forget, or we neglect it, or somehow our identities get hijacked by life, this world, or our self-delusion, the Spirit will call us back to the Lord Christ. The Spirit says your name is "champion." That's the way of the baptismal waters.

FOR REFLECTION

1. What are some mixed messages that you receive that might have hijacked your core identity of being a beloved child of God? What has that caused you to do?

2. Think about your own baptism or someone else's baptism you might have witnessed. Or if neither apply or you can't remember, think about the last time you were at the beach, at a lake, or a body of water. It's been said that going into the water means being buried with Christ, and rising or being lifted from the water means rising with Christ at his resurrection. What does it mean to die/rise with Christ as the continual pattern of our life?

3. For the gathered assembly when someone is being baptized, the gathered people of God are witnesses to the baptism, praying for the baptized, and also remembering and re-covenanting baptismal vows. What are you needing to recommit and re-covenant with God in your life?

PRAYER

From our mother's womb, to our birth, to now, living God, you have known us and our inward parts. Truly, in life and in death, we belong to you, faithful Lord. In baptism, Lord Christ, you give your church the gift of our belonging to you forever. Thank you for claiming us as your own, that being united in the death of your Son and in his risen and ascended life, we are given resurrection power and hope and freedom to live for you and to follow you. Set our course on life's pilgrimage, for as you accompany us and lead us and support us, may the journey be of joy because you are our North Star, our Provider, our Guide, our Purpose, our Creator. Amen.

3

JOY'S SPEECH

Wherefore when this Word of God is now preached in the church by preachers lawfully called, we believe that the very Word of God is proclaimed.

—Second Helvetic Confession (1561)[1]

Beware the demon of pomposity.

—Katharine Graham (1917–2001)

When Joy speaks, listen and follow. Daniel and I began our monthlong pilgrimage of the Camino Frances of the Camino de Santiago from the famed city of Saint-Jean-Pied-de-Port at the foot of the Pyrenees. We stayed at an *albergue* (hostel) called Le Chemin vers l'Étoile (the way to the star). The proprietor of that *albergue*, who had welcomed and housed thousands of *peregrinos* (pilgrims) over the years, offered five pieces of wisdom to us as we prepared to make our trek. He said:

- The camino is not a sprint but a marathon.
- You have nothing to prove to anyone.
- Everyone is sweaty and smelly—there's no pride on the camino.

1. Office of the General Assembly, *Book of Confessions*, §5.004, 77.

- If your body and soul say, take a rest, take a nap, get shade under tree... listen to your body and do it.
- Hydrate frequently.

Eric Viotte's sagacity proved to be true in every respect, and his wisdom is applicable not only on the Camino de Santiago, but also on the *camino de vida* (the road of life). I probably took his wisdom too closely to heart, for Daniel and I took every opportunity to sit under a tree, or take a nap on a bench, or stroll through wheat fields. My leisurely pace was too slow for my youthful companion, who grew impatient with me when I was sometimes one or two hours behind him.

Eric Viotte's timely wisdom is Joy's word for us. Every day we try to figure out what is in store for this slice of life for this season. One of the fruitful lessons of the COVID-19 pandemic was that while we may have a five- or ten-year plan for our lives, we have only today to live. Today, it may be enough to get out of bed and get dressed to see another day. For another person, today may mean a big meeting to share a PowerPoint presentation. Whatever today means for you, pay attention to what Joy's word is for you for this part of the journey. It becomes too overwhelming to see what Joy might be saying for what we hope our lives will be in ten or thirty years. But I have found that I am satisfied and content more when I work backwards. I reverse-engineer what the steps are that need to be done today in order to get to that end point. And even if the end point as I envisioned it today is not reached, at least the slice of what needs to be done today has been completed or is on the road to completion. For example, on the Camino de Santiago, when Daniel and I hiked on the first day about seventeen miles to Roncesvalles, Spain, from Saint-Jean-Pied-de-Port, we could see on the map where Roncesvalles was in relation to our starting point and we heard testimonies from other veteran pilgrims about their previous experiences. Based on all that information, we decided to wake up at 5:00 AM and begin our trek by 5:30 AM. As we ascended the first hill, with an incline that felt like ninety degrees, we said if we can get to the top of the hill by dawn, that will be an accomplishment for that morning. What we learned from Joy's word to us through Eric Viotte was that while the goal of that particular day was to get to Roncesvalles by the time the hostel closed at 9:00 PM, our camino for the first hour of that day was to wake up, get ready, and hike up a really steep hill. When we engage life in these slices, we enjoy the moment and do not rush to the next thing and the next adventure. Joy's word to us at the camino was that you eventually get to each point and place, but don't lose yourself in doing so. So being intentional about rest, paying attention to our mind-body-spirit, and delighting with fellow companions along the way enriched the camino, and, frankly, enriches all of life. By the way, we did arrive at Roncesvalles at about 7:00 PM (a whole fourteen-hour journey) on that first day. We did stop along the way to take photos with cows and sheep, and sat at a monument of rocks and pebbles where we added our message of hope to other pilgrims who traversed that route. What was key was to pay attention to Joy's word. What did Joy say that informs my life today on this slice of the journey?

Along the journey, we met different pilgrims from all walks of life—young and old; married, divorced, and single; Christian, non-Christian, and those of no faith—with various reasons for taking the pilgrimage. Some had a midlife crisis and wanted to discover themselves. A couple from Germany wanted to rekindle their love for one another after getting divorced and then remarried. In sharing their story, the wife even took the liberty of sharing about her husband's extramarital affair that led to their divorce! We met a vagabond who had left his home several months before as his family could not understand why he wanted to leave his job, let go of everything, and just enjoy the freedom of walking. He's probably still on one of the camino trails.

But regardless of the reason for being on the camino, Viotte's advice is helpful, both for walking the trail and for living, because the pilgrimage of our life and faith requires us to let go of our assumptions and follow the trail set before us. What is the baggage we carry that prevents us from fully following God, from loving God with all of our heart, soul, mind, and strength, and loving neighbors and strangers as we love ourselves? The so-called double love commandments, or the greatest commandments, are tall orders, but heeding Viotte's wisdom tells us several things about ourselves and the heart issues we grasp and cling to, which prevent us from traversing the pilgrimage of life with joy.

If you are anything like me, we need regular reminders of the wisdom that the camino is not a sprint but a marathon. We often fall prey to running through life, rushing to get to the next thing, seeing the present as though it consisted of perpetual stepping stones to the next stone, to the next pebble, rather than being fully present for the gift of the now. Yes, it's smelling the flowers along the road, and it's also watching the bee in the flower and maybe even risking being stung by the bee![2] Andy told me, following one of our times at the beach, that joy is being fully present in the now. When we do that, we fully internalize what is happening, where we

---

2. Wesley Granberg-Michaelson observed that accepting God's invitation "step by step, dropped oar by dropped oar" provides our mind with a chance to "catch its breath, or God's breath, setting forth to sail without oars . . . the walking pilgrim gradually leaves behind the distracted mind by physically leaving the spaces of those habitual distractions" (*Without Oars*, 39).

are, what we are feeling, what we are thinking. Joy is present. A billboard sign during the Christmas season that caught our attention recently put the matter succinctly: "The gift is the present."

The wisdom that we have nothing to prove to anyone goes alongside that first piece of wisdom. Why rush to the next town? You'll get there. Why run to Santiago de Compostela? There's no medal waiting for you, whether you get there at 2:00 or an hour later. At the risk of revealing my age to you, over the Christmas season in 2023, my high school classmates celebrated our thirtieth reunion. I couldn't attend, but seeing their photos on Facebook rekindled fond memories with many friends as we struggled through, survived in, and succeeded at Lowell High School. Those four years were fiercely competitive as each of us sought to build our college applications with as many extracurricular activities and advanced placement courses as possible. Class rank, the coveted Shield and Scroll honor society whose membership was determined by vote and invitation of peers, and sharing through the grapevine which colleges each of us were accepted or rejected from—these were many of the hallmarks of our high school years. But in retrospect, none of that matters. It mattered to us in the moment, of course, but it doesn't really in the end. Looking at the photos of our thirtieth high school reunion, I regret that I didn't get to enjoy more of the others in our class of 667 students. Lowell High School drilled into us the lesson to be disciplined with our schedule and to stay focused on the imminent college admissions process, which left precious little time for socializing. So we focused on the few in our circles, in our classes, and in our various activities. If I could go back in time and preach a word to my younger self, or better yet, if I could travel to Lowell High School and tell the current classes one message, it would be this: don't rush things, and enjoy those who journey with you, because in the end, all this competition doesn't really matter.

A subset of that piece of wisdom is the next one: there's no pride on the camino because everyone is sweaty and smelly. Part of pride is comparing oneself to others, and part of that comparison is coveting, shame, or malcontent. Viotte's wisdom is right on target in speaking truth that you and I and every pilgrim are sweaty and dirty from the dusty roads, hiking the rough terrain for hours on end, sometimes skipping a shower because you are fatigued and just want to sleep when you arrive at the next village. There's no pride, or there ought to be no pride, because we are in the same lot. You could be a millionaire, and no one would know that; even if they did, it wouldn't help you because we're all hiking the same road and are walking to the same destination. Having money or a title or an academic degree doesn't give you any advantage on the camino. Granted, on the camino of life, there are sadly great inequalities and inequities. But the lesson of the

Camino de Santiago expresses what would it be like if life were like that—regardless of socioeconomic class or birthplace, we all are on the same road with no added advantage.

It's the nature of the "ought" and the "should" that awakened for me what joy's duty is and what joy's word is to us. While it's true that there ought not be an added advantage on the camino because all of us are dirty and sweaty, in reality there are many who have advantage in this world because of their birthplace, intergenerational wealth, skin pigmentation, and various other factors. And while it's true that we should not feel pride as we are on life's journey, and wisdom's words in the ancient book of Ecclesiastes remind us that life is "vanity of vanities" and all of us will meet our certain death, it is in our human nature to feel pride with regard to both neighbor and stranger. Taking Viotte's prescription for the camino and reflecting upon it in retrospect inspired me to see how joy's word is a call to make right the broad chasm that exists on the journey. While all human beings are on a journey where we all will die someday, the reality of the journey itself is that some sweat more than others; some will get dirtier and dustier than others or will stay dirty and dusty longer. We may all be heading to San Francisco, but some may be able only to drive the ten hours on Interstate 5 and not have the resources to take a private jet that cuts that time to one hour. Of course, such a statement presumes that there's more joy in the ease of the journey—the private jet versus the ten-hour car ride—than in the journey itself.

Are joy's call and responsibility to work towards a world where everyone must be on the same level of having to trek the ten-hour car ride to San Francisco? Or are they that everyone should be given the resources to be able to fly the private jet? Or is it joy's call to work for a world where everyone has the resources and, therefore, the option to choose whether they wish to exercise their agency to take the ten-hour car ride or the private jet? Upon reflection, it seems that Joy's call and responsibility are to provide the conditions, environment, and opportunity where all people can dignify all people as fellow pilgrims on that same journey. At a recent Aspen Security Forum gathering, US Secretary of State Antony Blinken was asked what his final advice would be for a new generation of policymakers and diplomats. He said: "I think that the most potent poison in our common wealth is dehumanization, the inability to see the humanity in someone else." He added that the consequences of dehumanization are the following: "Everything good becomes so much harder, everything bad becomes so much more possible."[3] When we regard neighbors and strangers alike as fellow human travelers, that is a game changer in our human relationships and

---

3. Blinken, "Secretary Blinken Participates," 41:28–41:40.

that is the first step and essential factor on the road to justice. We can't even begin to talk about providing equal opportunities to access to resources if our possible conversation partners don't dignify all other travelers as fellow human beings. If we engage with one another with the foundational notion that we see the humanity in one another, then we can probe why it is that so many don't have access to resources to even have the agency and option to walk, drive, or fly to San Francisco. The converse is true. If we dehumanize one another or diminish another person's humanity, then we won't care about equality nor equity. To dehumanize another person or to diminish another person's humanity makes us less than human. It is antihuman, it is inhuman. In other words, we lose our humanity and our sense of true self. This means, when we engage in injustice or don't attend to justice for all people, we are less human and we become impoverished of joy. This is what the Psalm 51 text described as needing a "generous spirit."

Viotte's wisdom of paying attention to our bodies is Joy's word that prods us to pay attention to our own humanity. My wife shared a nugget of wisdom from an anonymous writer: "We are human beings, not human doings." The Protestant work ethic, economics since the Industrial Revolution, and the digital revolution with the ubiquity of machine learning and artificial intelligence all express a goal for maximal efficiency and optimal productivity. Society and politics value humans for what a fellow human being can do towards the profit margin or the financial bottom line. So when we regard human beings that way, we fall prey to that mindset and it becomes what I call a heart-set and a soul-set. We constantly do, constantly produce, are constantly on the move; we do so to the detriment and peril of our mind-body-soul. Joy's word to us through Viotte is: pay attention to your mind-body-soul. Are you treating your own self the way you regard other human beings?

It's ironic that this is the last chapter I am writing in this book. I skipped around in writing, and it turned out that this particular chapter is the last one. As I type this sentence, I am under a deadline to the publisher to finish this even though my body says it is time to sleep. On the Camino de Santiago, I exercised my freedom to listen to my feet and aching legs and to slow down my pace, or to sit at the side of the road and just catch a breath. I even took the occasion once to sit next to a group of stray cats who were hanging around a fountain and give them some morsels of a baguette I had in my pack. Listening to our bodies will save us much pain and hardship later. Those of us in the Reformed tradition belong to a household of theological practice where we give such pride of place to the mind, the intellect, and learning. We won't rehearse the history of a time in the nineteenth century when Presbyterians split over the frontier of the expanding United States and the necessity of a learned clergy educated and trained in theological seminaries. Yet we live at our peril if we don't pay attention to our bodies; or, more accurately, if we live as unintegrated selves: mind, body, and heart existing as separate entities.[4] To pay attention to our bodies' needs is to care for our minds and our souls; it's impossible to separate one part from the other.

Finally, turning to Eric Viotte's final piece of wisdom to hydrate frequently—that is lifelong and lifetime wisdom, because without water and without the Water of Life, we are dead. But note this: when we feel the sensation of thirst, our bodies were actually thirsty long ago, so that by the time the pang for a jug of water comes to mind, our bodies have already been needing hydration for an hour or two. So it is important to preempt the thirst sensation by drinking at least every twenty minutes on a strenuous pilgrimage as the Camino de Santiago. This goes to show, too, that on the camino of life, we need to attend to the health of our bodies and souls continually, not only when we feel the pain of neglect.

What prevents us from doing all this? What are the obstacles that keep us from following the wisdom of the camino? The late Katharine Graham, publisher of *The Washington Post*, wrote to journalist Bob Woodward when he and co-journalist Carl Bernstein broke the Watergate scandal. After several years of their having followed leads that others were disbelieving, leads that seemed like irrelevant rabbit trails to others, Nixon's resignation proved Woodward and Bernstein right—that they had followed the evidence towards the truth, even when that truth led to the highest office of the United States. Graham jotted down the following words to Woodward: "Beware the demon of pomposity."[5]

Graham wasn't a preacher nor a theologian by any stretch of the imagination, but her word was a sermon worth preaching. Our hearts need truth, because without truth, we will not experience the joy of God's salvation. The God of truth is our joy, the living God who is our Joy delights in truth. In the living God there is no prevarication, no shadow of turning; the One who in the Ten Commandments says, "You shall not bear false witness," desires that we not bear false witness because God does not bear false witness. God's yes means yes, and God's no means no.

Human pomposity and human pride desire for hegemony and authority. We seek control over our tongues, our bodies, our decisions, our choices, our relationships, our beliefs, our attitudes, our habits. No matter how destructive towards others and ourselves, our tendency is to cling to

---

4. See Presa, "Stewardship of Mind."

5. Woodward recounted this at an event our family attended at the Balboa Theater in downtown San Diego on August 14, 2022.

ourselves and our notion of yes and no. We are stubborn—hardheaded and hard-hearted—in that we cling to our way of doing things rather than submitting to the humility of the camino wisdom. We may hear Joy's word for us, but we refuse to enact it.

Joy's speech is the antidote to our proclivity to listen to ourselves, or to listen to other authorities whose words are not wisdom at all. Such words may not be life giving, joy restoring, love granting.

When the people of God gather around the Word, the Spirit prepares our hearts through preparatory songs, hymns, psalms, a prayer of confession, an assurance of pardon, the reading and hearing of sacred Scripture. The Spirit of God uses these sacred elements to summon our hearts, to prime our ears to hear what the Lord has to say. There comes a time for interpretation and exposition of the Word, when a human being called by God to speak Joy's truth to us will arrive on the scene and will testify to truth. It's in those moments that Joy proclaims God's love. Joy will herald the story of how our Sovereign was victorious in battle against the enemy. Joy will speak good news to the bad news that has inundated our living days. The Spirit transforms the words to the Word because the truth that is proclaimed is connected to the living Word. The Word proclaimed is from the One who is resurrected and ascended, the One by whose Spirit we are awakened, enlivened, transformed, reassured of God's love.

The preaching of the Word is a sacred task. Offering holy speech is a holy vocation. It has been a primary means by which the oracles of God have been shared. Proclamation concerns the covenantal accounts of God's historic faithfulness being recounted for generations. It is through the proclamation of the Word that sin is confronted and God's people are encouraged to participate in God's vision for humanity. It's in and through proclamation that we catch a glimpse of the unfolding and emerging *eschaton*. The real stuff of life begins to emerge: God's world, where forgiveness is possible and is, in fact, given; where grace and goodness are not sound bites but actual realities of transformed lives demonstrating God's love. Preaching is God's revolution against powers and principalities that claim an authority over our lives. When we receive the preached Word, we are reminded that our lives are reserved for God and God's prerogatives. We belong to the One who made us, after all. Joylessness and despair reign so prevalent in our lives and in this world because we have allowed other voices to have authority and free rein over our lives. We have succumbed to competing voices rather than the gifts of love, joy, peace, patience, and all the fruit of the Spirit (Gal 5:22–23).

Preaching is a distinctive form of speech and rhetoric. While similar to rhetoric, preaching has a paraenetic quality. The power of preaching relies not so much on the methods of the preacher nor on the preacher herself—although good methods and an engaging preacher are helpful. Rather, the efficacy comes from the work of the Spirit of God. The preacher, with all the sophistication of rhetorical skills, sound exegesis, and structured homiletics can help to deliver a clear, crisp, organized sermon. As a preaching professor, I advise my students that those tools are means by which the One who is our Joy speaks, convicts, persuades, and transforms hearts. One homiletical style or a raised tone or vocal cadence in and of themselves won't turn a sinner into saint, but when the Spirit of God uses that cadence or that exegetical point to transform hearts, it is because that cadence and exegetical point were attached to some truth of the Scriptures about the Lord Christ. Perhaps that point of emphasis or that commentary on that Bible verse was about God's saving act in the exodus or the exile, or about the cross and the empty tomb. Then we can see that the Spirit's action hinges on the gospel itself, the faithful attestation of that central act of Christ that pivots the message from a mere rhetorical, theatrical performance to a sacred arena of the living God addressing human hearts to confess Jesus is Lord.

In doing so, the Spirit of Christ specially uses the speech act of preaching to recalibrate and reanchor our lives. The Spirit transforms our disposition, attitudes, priorities, and decisions towards that of the triune God, the One who is our Joy, and, consequently, we experience the joy of God's salvation.

In the Presbyterian Church (U.S.A.), we articulate the depth and breadth of proclamation as theological act. The Second Helvetic Confession asserts that "Scripture is the Word of God"[6] and that the "preaching of the Word of God is the Word of God."[7] This, of course, does not suggest that the written text of Scripture nor the act of proclamation are somehow extra persons of the triune God, with the living Christ as the eternal Word (John 1:1). This multidimensional understanding of "Word of God" or speech of God was captured by the Confession of 1967 (C67). In that statement of faith, C67 confessed that:

> The one sufficient revelation of God is Jesus Christ, the Word of God incarnate, to whom the Holy Spirit bears unique and authoritative witness through the Holy Scriptures, which are received and obeyed as the word of God written. The Scriptures are not a witness among others, but the witness without parallel. The church has received the books of the Old and New Testaments as prophetic and apostolic testimony in which it

---

6. Office of the General Assembly, *Book of Confessions*, §5.003, 77.
7. Office of the General Assembly, *Book of Confessions*, §5.004, 77.

hears the word of God and by which its faith and obedience are nourished and regulated.[8]

The thick description of what is understood as speech of God, breath of God, Word of God is summarily expressed in the constitutional questions propounded to those being ordained, installed, or commissioned. The second question asks: "Do you accept the Scriptures of the Old and New Testament to be, by the Holy Spirit, the unique and authoritative witness to Jesus Christ in the Church universal, and God's Word to you?"[9] C67 is careful to use uppercase *w* and lowercase *w* to distinguish between the living Word incarnate, Jesus Christ who is the eternally begotten Son of God, and the mediated words (Scripture, preaching/proclamation) that attest to the living Word incarnate. But C67 seeks to locate the presence of the Word of God whenever and wherever the Holy Spirit is in tandem with the reading and hearing of Scripture or in the proclamation and hearing of preaching/proclamation. We recall the pivotal significance Calvin placed on the role of the Holy Spirit in his 1542 liturgy for the Genevan church. Calvin believed the lynchpin of worship is the presence and power of the Holy Spirit, whom the gathered assembly invokes in the "prayer for illumination." The Reformed theological traditions hold to the belief that human hearts and minds cannot comprehend nor accept nor follow the Word of God unless and until the Holy Spirit's perspicacious work opens up our lives and our understanding to receive the Word. The Presbyterian Church (U.S.A.)'s Directory for Worship summarizes this belief:

> A prayer for illumination calls on the Holy Spirit to empower the reading, understanding, proclaiming, and living of God's Word. This sense of utter reliance on the illumination of the Spirit is an important and distinctive mark of the Reformed tradition. The prayer for illumination precedes the reading of Scripture and preaching of the sermon and applies to all of the readings, as well as the proclamation of the Word.[10]

The reliance upon the power, presence, and person of the Holy Spirit in instantiating the efficacy of God's Word carries over in Calvin's view of the centrality of that part of the eucharistic liturgy dialogue called the *Sursum Corda* (Lift up your hearts). I will take up this piece in the subsequent chapter on the Lord's Table. But for the point here, the Reformed theological traditions underline the necessity of the Holy Spirit to make what may seem

---

8. Office of the General Assembly, *Book of Confessions*, §9.27, 291.
9. Office of the General Assembly, *Constitution 2019–2023*, W-4.0404a, 104.
10. Office of the General Assembly, *Constitution 2019–2023*, W-3.0302, 90.

like ordinary words being proclaimed to become the Word of God upon the hearers and receivers of that word that is being read and proclaimed.

The provenance of the authoritative character of the Word is God's self, who is Joy embodied and incarnate. Why does proclamation/preaching demand our attention and our obedience, and the silencing (or at least lowering the volume of all others) of other so-called voices of authority? Because our lives are restless unless and until the Word of our Creator is speaking to the inner recesses of our being in a way that no one else and nothing else can do.

In the Filipino culture, the eldest son is expected to be an attorney, a medical doctor, or an engineer. Throughout high school, I aspired to be a medical surgeon. When asked which type of surgeon, I answered, "Whichever makes the most money." I enrolled at the University of California, Davis, as a biochemistry major. Little did I know that freshman organic chemistry is the winnowing class to see who really is meant to traverse the journey of the hard sciences. After two weeks of organic chem, I dropped the class, and with that I dropped the dream. I was a C-SPAN junkie and loved watching the live debates and committee hearings of the US Congress, especially of the US Senate. So, perusing the academic catalog, I landed on political science and history. Had I known Craig Barnes (president emeritus of Princeton Theological Seminary) as a friend and mentor when I was an undergraduate freshman, he would have said, "Neal, your major does not and will not determine the rest of your life." This is advice Craig has preached to college and seminary students alike. How true that word is!

I spent the next four years of college digging deep into my two college majors. I loved every class in the political science and history departments. My work led me to an internship at the flagship San Francisco field office of the late US Senator Dianne Feinstein, who had been elected to the Senate as California's senior senator a few years prior. As graduation was approaching, I planned to go to law school and do a joint JD/PhD. I wanted to be able to teach and practice national security law, work for the US Senate Foreign Relations Committee. But my dreams did not stop there. I wanted to run for the US House of Representatives, specifically for the congressional district I had known while growing up. That is what I planned. That is what I aspired to do.

The wisdom of God is true and trustworthy when it says, "The human mind plans the way, but the Lord directs the steps" (Prov 16:9). My story took a turn when confronted with the word of God, which directed me to the Word of God. When my pastor took our choir director and me to then Whitworth College (now Whitworth University located in Spokane, Washington) for their annual Institute for Ministry, the guest preacher for the week was the president of San Francisco Theological Seminary. A skilled orator, pastor, and preacher, the Rev. Dr. Donald McCullough was well read in literature, poetry, the arts, theology, and, of course, the Bible. But it wasn't his oratorical skills nor his eloquent storytelling that captivated my attention. It was as if his sermon was speaking directly to me. In that weeklong event where Don was the daily preacher, the one particular sermon that hit me was when he preached from Matthew 9:37, "The harvest is plentiful, but the laborers are few."

The Spirit of the Lord speaks to the heart like no one else can. I had heard that verse before, but I hadn't listened to that verse until that moment. The Spirit, in partnership with that word and Don as preacher and Whitworth College as the setting, was my Senate-directed heart's existential threat. What I had planned, what I had conceived, what I had strategized for were about to be hijacked by the living God. It was soul wrenching. My pastor could sense it. He could see I was bothered by the Word. Throughout the rest of the conference, I would get teary eyed during the prayer time. It felt as if my chest was being opened and my heart and insides were being pulled out.

The word of God and the Word of God confronted me with a hard question: "Neal, why do you want to go to law school?" My answer in prayer was that law school would enable me to have a career in the foreign policy committee of Congress and then run for a seat in Congress.

But the Spirit of the living God was not satisfied with that response because I was withholding the extent of the truth. The Spirit of God was inviting me to finish the sentence. I wanted to go to Congress because I loved the power and attention that came with being an elected member of Congress, just as I saw on C-SPAN and just as I experienced in my little world of being a student senator at UC Davis. There it is. That was what I wanted. It wasn't to use the position to address human suffering, poverty, and war. It wasn't to curb drugs or improve our roads and bridges. It was so that I could rise in the ranks, earn a committee chairmanship, steer appropriations funds to the district, be a part of ribbon-cutting ceremonies, make speeches, raise money, run for the US Senate, and do it all over again but on a larger scale. In reflecting upon that truth, that internalized illusion of joy, I felt terrible, joyless, and raw.

No, I want to be a laborer in the kingdom. Lord Jesus, I want to be a teacher of theology. I want to be in ministry, to serve you and your people full-time. That's what I prayed. And that's what I struggled with.

When we returned to California, I shared my newfound revelation. My immediate family, with the exception of my maternal grandmother, said that maybe I was just excited about the conference. They advised to give it a week and see what happens. My maternal grandmother, who was an avid church attendee and Bible study teacher, was joyful. She had prayed that this would happen. My paternal grandparents were not as excited; my paternal grandmother, who is a conservative Roman Catholic, was not pleased at all. Because my father is their only son and I am his only son, then in the patrilineal character of Filipino culture, the Presa family name continues through him and through me. To my paternal grandma, switching from law school to ministry meant the priesthood. And in her mind and heart, priesthood meant celibacy, which meant the Presa family name would become extinct with me.

The cultural expectations pressed on every side, as did my own self-doubt. I wondered for several months if what I felt and heard at Whitworth was the Spirit's voice or my internal fear of what law school and a life in elected public service might entail. Maybe it was the intensity of four years of college and working so hard to excel in all my studies that was getting to me and I needed a long vacation, perhaps a backpacking trip across Europe.

Through several months of praying—by my family by blood and by my church family by water—I listened for the Spirit's convicting voice. The Word of God through the word of God, who spoke through Don's sermon, reverberated in my heart and soul again. It was a joyous word. It was an act of joy that freed me from the fear of letting go of the plans I had laid out for law school, and to take the risk of applying to seminary.

By the time of the senior luncheon of the department of political science, I knew what to share with my fellow classmates and professors. One by one we were invited to stand and briefly say a word about our plans after graduation. My colleagues each said, "Law school." "Work at the Capitol." "Internship." "Graduate school in political science." "Law school." "Law school." When it came around to me, I stood up. "Seminary. I'm going to seminary for a master of divinity." I felt deep joy mixed with doubt as I shared this news with colleagues who had expected something different from me.

Rowan Williams, former archbishop of Canterbury, remarked that theological education "is learning more about the world that faith creates, or the world that faith trains you to inhabit."[11] Such a descriptor can also apply to what preaching and proclamation of the Word does: proclamation apprentices and attunes our lives to Joy, encoding upon our existential DNA the people we are created to be. Preaching is the Spirit echoing into the caverns and pockets of our lives where stalactites and stalagmites are calcifying life and joy. Preaching sweeps away the grime and dust that have settled in our hearts so that we can more freely live in the joy of God's salvation and experience the cosmological consequence of doing so. In short, preaching

---

11. Wayman, "Rowan Williams," para. 3.

widens, deepens, and broadens our horizons to the world on the other side of the wardrobe to Narnia, where wild adventures await and where the joyous wonder of living in and with the Lord is our present and our future.

One important word needs to be said about a dimension of "word" that I've referenced in this chapter and in every place I talk about preaching. That word is the word of "prayer." So much of what I've written here has focused on preaching and the proclamation of the Word, which bears witness to the living Word, Jesus the Christ, our Joy. This past academic year teaching at Fuller Theological Seminary, we in the preaching faculty began an experiment in the curriculum. For a whole year, we revised the required MDiv class on "Introduction to Preaching/Homiletics" and integrated it into the elective class on "Introduction to Christian Worship," making it one class, "Introduction to Preaching and Worship." The premise of this approach is commonsense and readily apparent: preaching is an event that occurs in and because of the context of worship. Preaching and worship are not disparate, disconnected events; they are like hand-in-glove partners in the business of expressing and embodying God's love with the latter (worship) providing the contextual framework for the former (preaching). The Spirit convicts us of the efficacy of preaching in the context of worship through prayer.

Prayer as word, prayer as a language medium through which and in which bilateral communication occurs between God and us, transforms and convicts. Yes, in prayer we offer our individual and communal hopes, fears, petitions, and praises to God for ourselves and this world. But more than cascading our intercessions and thanksgiving in a unilateral, unidirectional fashion from us to God, prayer as word has a preeminent function in that the living God is conversing with us.

As we are praying and as we are prompted to pray, the Spirit of the living God is doing a mighty work upon our hearts and minds. The words we utter are given by the Spirit of God. The prayers we pray for loved ones, strangers, peoples and lands halfway around the world, the flourishing of planet Earth—these promptings upon the heart are guided by the Spirit of God who cares deeply about each of those persons and places. My pastor colleague, Greg Bostrom of Christ Presbyterian Church, La Costa, in Carlsbad, California, recently preached from the lectionary text in Luke 2 on the final Sunday in 2023, wherein Simeon and Anna prophesied over Mary and the baby Jesus in the temple. Greg reminded us, as with the ancient prophecy, that God pierces our souls and hearts with the Lord's "full and fierce love." The living God uses the word of prayer to express God's full and fierce love for us and for the world. God uses the word of prayer to transform our hearts to view ourselves, the world around us, and God's self through the lens of God's own heart.

Shortly after the horrific attack of Hamas upon Israel on October 7, 2023, and the ensuing and still ongoing war between Israel and Hamas in Gaza, my ministry colleague Laura Cheifetz posted a prayer on Facebook. The prayer she penned was four days after the attack. But those four days were enough for the world to witness the utter devastation wreaked by each side—thousands killed, hundreds of thousands displaced from their homes, a couple hundred taken as hostages, towns razed to the ground, and a burgeoning humanitarian crisis that has no end in sight. Laura's prayer is a word to us and for us, a word which our hearts speak, a word from us:

> A blessing.
> We gather here in this cathedral of sky and trees
> a temple carpeted with grass and dirt
> our hearts crying out to all that is holy.
> We grieve the tragedies, the betrayals,
> the deep hurt that bring us together.
> Even in our confusion, pain, and rage, and worst of all,
> our resignation and despair,
> we are still carrying hope.
> It is tender, battered, and afraid, but it lives in us still.
> hope, remembering what our ancestors survived
> hope, that in mourning we are not alone
> hope, because in a community, we can take turns carrying
> the burden of being part of a broken world.
> May we marry our imperfect hope with
> our anger in such a way that
> we are propelled into relationship
> seeking justice, not retribution
> fueling our desire to heal instead of hurt
> hold instead of hate
> create beauty rather than resentment
> because what is life but an opportunity to bring love
> to all the world.
> May we leave here to be
> tenacious
> tender-hearted
> clear-headed
> focused
> full of wonder
> and committed to a just peace
> in all places for all created beings.

> This is not a call to forget
> or pretend or ignore
> but an invitation to create
> the world we all deserve
> lush + gentle + forgiving
> from the inside out.
> Everything starts somewhere. Perhaps we might start here.
> May it be so.[12]

FOR REFLECTION

1. What word are you needing or desiring to hear from the Spirit of the Lord?

2. When was the last time you heard and received a sermon that truly convicted you and moved you to act and where you beheld the glory of God? What was it in that sermon or about that sermon that drew that response from you?

3. What word from God do you want to share and proclaim to your loved ones, to strangers, and to the world? What word are they needing to hear?

PRAYER

Alpha and Omega, your speech was the first, and from you came light and all of creation, and your speech will be the last. Speak to us in a way that only you can. Declare to us your truth that transforms hearts, that conforms wills to your own, that forms and sustains faith, that convicts us of our need of your mercy and grace in Christ, that reassures us that we belong to you. You alone are our joy, so when you speak, faithful Lord, you make us glad, for there is no other Word but yours. So, beckon us continually on life's pilgrimage lest we fall or wander away. When we do, pursue us, call us, and never let us go. Teach us your way, and set our path to follow you, the One and the same, Jesus the Christ. Amen.

---

12. Vigil, closing benediction, 2023. Prayer printed by permission of the Rev. Laura Mariko Cheifetz.

4

JOY'S FEAST

The only real fall of man is his noneucharistic
life in a noneucharistic world.
—Fr. Alexander Schmemann[1]

He took the Who's feast, he took the Who pudding, he took the roast beast.
He cleaned out that ice box as quick as a flash.
Why, the Grinch even took their last can of Who hash.
—Dr. Seuss

You serve me a six-course dinner / right in front of my enemies.
You revive my drooping head; / my cup brims with blessing.
—Psalm 23:5 MSG

Joy doesn't eat. Joy doesn't dine. Joy feasts.
    A common invitation to the Lord's Table is these words from the Gospel according to Luke:

---

1. Schmemann, *For the Life*, 18.

> Friends, this is the joyful feast of the people of God! They will come from east and west and from north and south, and sit at table in the kingdom of God. According to Luke, when our risen Lord was at table with his disciples, he took the bread, and blessed and broke it, and gave it to them. Then their eyes were opened and they recognized him. This is the Lord's table. Our Savior invites those who trust him to share the feast which he has prepared.[2]

And that it should be, a joyful feast. Always, in every way and in every time.

"So, I pondered, why is communion somber, staid, and almost melancholic, as if we were at a funeral, when this should be a joyful feast?" I reflected upon that question for many months when my pastor colleague and I, as the two associate pastors of Village Church, were assigned to complete the eucharistic liturgy following our colleague, the senior pastor, who pronounced the invitation to the Table. She and I would approach the round eucharistic Table, with all four hundred congregants' eyes focused on us, as one offered a pastoral prayer of thanksgiving, followed by the other lifting the bread while saying the words of institution and then breaking the bread. Then the other would lift the chalice containing fruit of the vine and close with "These are the gifts of God for the people of God."

Once this liturgy was complete, our job was to stand behind the Table and wait for about ten minutes while the elders and deacons served the congregation row by row. Maybe we would glance at each seated parishioner as the tray was passed along their row. Mostly we stood in somber silence. It would seem creepy, I thought, if we smiled the whole time.

So, one Sunday, I decided to change things up a bit. Because no one, apart from us and the Lord, knows what is on the Table, I decided to print out a big smiley face on a piece of paper and placed it in my Bible. When we went up to the Table after the servers were serving the wafer tray, I took out that smiley face and directed my colleague's attention to it, and, boy, did she chuckle and laugh. When I sensed that she or I were falling into the usual posture of Rev. Melancholy or Rev. Stiff Lip, I pointed to that smiley face again and we had a joyful feast. None of the congregants really responded to our laughter or our bigger smiles. There was still a stoic sense in the sanctuary as congregants seemed to want to retain the silence, except for the organ, which played a background song. Silence was equated with solemnity. For us, though, we as preachers had a chuckle, a playful laughter. It was a moment of joy with Joy as we served the people of God.

---

2. Presbyterian Church (U.S.A.), *Book of Common Worship*, 68.

When I had the privilege, pleasure, and blessing of serving as moderator of the 220th General Assembly of the Presbyterian Church (U.S.A.) from 2012 to 2014, one of my stump speeches was to talk about the difference between eating, dining, and feasting. Eating is the action of putting food in your mouth, which anyone of any age can do. Dining is eating but with table manners, using utensils, behaving at the table, keeping quiet conversation so as not to disturb fellow diners. Feasting, on the other hand, is about having a party, welcoming all people, laughing boisterously, telling stories, singing, and bringing your whole self to the table. Your family's joys, hurts, challenges, failures, and achievements are all gladly received at a feast. Feasting is focused on the relationships around the table, the experience of being together, of belonging to one another. Neighbors and strangers alike are all welcome. And feasting is about abundance—an abundance of food, abundance of generous welcome, abundance of making all feel they belong, as if they have known each other all their lives. Feasting is about the abundance of joyous thanksgiving.

I'm going to tap three academic disciplines for a moment, because they each have something particular to teach us about the wonderful dynamic of joyful feasts and the feast of Joy of the eucharistic Table. The academic disciplines are phenomenology, ritual studies, and anthropology. In a nutshell, here's what can be said about feasts from the perspective of these three disciplines:

- Meaning is created and cultivated by people gathering with one another around food.
- The action of gathering around table, or around food, is constitutive of human culture.
- Sharing—giving to and receiving from one another—is essential to understanding what it means to be human.
- Humans who see infants and younger people being welcomed and cared for by older humans receive a clear message that we belong to a tribe/culture/clan that values all ages.
- Storytelling is the currency and the lifeblood of community.
- Deep gratitude is cultivated at table.

The most indelible mark I have from my childhood are the sights, smells, sounds, and tastes of excellent cooking and delicious Filipino food from my parents, paternal grandmother, maternal grandmother, aunts, and uncles. Whether it was chicken adobo, beef *nilaga* soup, fried fish, garlic fried rice, *kare-kare* (peanut butter oxtail stew), baked trout, fried eggs, or my

Mama Pacing's famed mocha cake, our weekly family gatherings and special occasion parties were sights to behold because of the sheer variety of our cuisine, the amount of effort to make it, and the enjoyment of all who partook.

Every year, after our midnight Christmas Eve Mass at St. Mary's Cathedral in San Francisco, my parents would cook a pot full of *calandracas*, a chicken-based soup of *mirepoix* and noodles flavored with a hint of fish sauce popular in my father's hometown of Cavite in the Philippines. This soup was paired with a toasted *pan de sal* bread with butter. This would be followed by opening presents and singing Christmas carols.

As a child and an adolescent, the feasting table was connected with joy and with the worship at the Table, the Lord's Table that we experienced at church worship service, and which was connected to our family's dinner table. When I was a child and an adolescent, I identified the midnight Mass and the Lord's Table with our family's dinner afterward, because in both settings we were thankful and we were joyful. Because we always said mealtime prayers, even at our large family parties and gatherings, faith was feasting and feasting was faith; or to put it more accurately, when we were feasting, we were worshipping.

Earl Palmer, a longtime Presbyterian pastor, facilitated a Bible study at a Wee Kirk Conference I attended many years ago. In it, he broke down for us the etymology of the word "Eucharist": *chara* is the Greek word for joy, which means a surprise; *charis* is the Greek word for grace, which is a surprising gift. He pointed out how *charismata* is the Greek word used in 1 Corinthians 12 to describe "spiritual gifts." As joy (*chara*) and grace (*charis*) are similar, he pointed out how putting those two together shows us that joy is a surprising gift. Then, he added, the prefix *eu* (the Greek letters epsilon and upsilon) means "good." Eulogy, for example, or *eu* plus logos, is a good word about a deceased person. So, *eu* plus *charis*, or Eucharist, is a good surprising gift. The Greek word used in the New Testament for thanksgiving is *eucharistia*, or a good gift of joy. Thus, the Eucharist is the table feast of thanksgiving for God's good surprise gift, namely Jesus the Christ.

I used to enjoy watching Food Network, especially the food challenges where home cooks compete under time constraints. At some point, though, knowing of so many communities around the world and having visited poverty-stricken communities in the Philippines, Lebanon, Cuba, Guyana, Trinidad, and other places around the world and in the United States, I could not subscribe to viewing the wastefulness of those type of shows. I imagined how a hungry young person and their family might respond if they heard a Food Network judge complaining, "You didn't put a parsley garnish on that steak!" I was brought up not to be wasteful with even a grain of rice, because in the Philippines we were very aware of how much care it took for a rice farmer and their family to tend to rice crops, making grain precious. And having prepared many of the Filipino dishes I enjoyed as a child, I well appreciate the time and effort it takes to slice and dice every vegetable, every piece of onion and garlic, and sauté them over a hot stove for my family to enjoy. That's how I was brought up, to be thankful for each meal and the hands that prepared it. This attention and gratitude are acts of devotion to God—they bring joy, they are joy.[3]

Joy and thanksgiving are inextricably linked. They aren't two sides of the same coin but more than that; joy and thanksgiving are like an alloy of two bonded metals constituting love. When we give thanks—to God, to neighbor and stranger—we recognize our connection with a fellow person and their connection with us. From a restaurant server giving you a glass of water, to a parent giving help for their child's homework, to you saying thank you to God for shelter from the storm. Gratitude is a recognition that our existence matters, that we are not alone. Joy is the state, condition, emotion, and experience of being awakened with that recognition of belonging. We belong not to ourselves alone, but to our Creator, and to other persons. If we lived on an isolated island and awakened to each day, there would be gratitude for being alive, but we would begin to miss human interaction. I think of Tom Hanks's movie *Cast Away* when Hanks's character was filled with deep gratitude and joy, awakening on an island after the FedEx plane on which he had flown had crashed into the ocean, but he'd survived. But after many weeks of being on that island, his joy dissipated. Even though he had monologues with Wilson, a soccer ball he had found in the wreckage and which was of the Wilson athletic brand, his initial joy of having survived the crash disappeared as the time continued without another living person.[4] But when we are able to interact with persons—God and humans—on a positive level, there is gratitude. And with that, there is an element of joy and an element of love.

For many Christian ecclesial traditions, the Eucharist–Lord's Table–communion is the apex, the summit of Christian worship; it is worship. For our Orthodox siblings, the Table is sacramentally the joining of heaven and earth, when the gathered assembly is mysteriously joined to the ascended Christ and the life of the triune community in a heavenly dimension. For

---

3. I am grateful to Kenda Creasy Dean, who insightfully described "domain arenas" as sacred spaces where young adults discover meaning and belonging, not necessarily in church sanctuaries but in what she calls "alternative spatial communities." For my growing-up years, my family's kitchen and the dining table and my extended families' kitchens were the "domain arenas," the "alternative spatial communities." Personal conversation on March 4, 2022.

4. Zemeckis, *Cast Away*.

our Catholic siblings, the Table is the Mass; it is the repeated self-giving of the Lord Jesus Christ for the sins of the world. For us Reformed, the Spirit of Christ *trans-elements* us, renewing us and changing us because anyone and anything whom the Lord encounters is changed in an unseen way.[5] We cannot help but be changed when we are in the presence of God, in the presence of the gifts of God for the people of God. Eucharist–Lord's Table–communion unites us to God and to people beyond and including all those who gathered in that immediate space.

Where baptism is our initiation into the body of Christ, the starting point of the journey as a child of God, the eucharistic Table of thanksgiving is the repeated feast. The Eucharist–Lord's Table–communion is where God's children are nourished and fed. This is where we are continually joined and in communion with the ascended Christ in the unity and fellowship of the Spirit. It is the ascended Christ who also unites us to all of God's people in every time and in every place. Thus, every eucharistic celebration is a community gathering of the faithful. It is a convening of both the living and those who have died in the Lord.

There is joy and thanksgiving at the eucharistic Table because it is the Lord's Table that Christ sets, which he has established. Jesus Christ desires that we meet him and his friends there. We are counted as God's beloved friends. He yearns to be with us, to give of himself, to share his life, to share who he is with us. What a blessing, what a privilege, what a gift! To have our Savior, our Lord, the One through whom all creation came to desire to feast with us. So great is his love for us that it is said when we receive the sacrament, "Take, eat, this is my body given for you." This is intimate communion with the Lord. The Lord freely shares with us. Christ unites us with him that we are, sacramentally speaking, eating and drinking of his body and of his blood. The outward orientation of the triune God draws us outward, too, oriented with outstretched arms to the world for which God gave his Son, Jesus Christ.[6]

While our family feasts are prepared with certain family in mind at the moment, the notion of family shifts as the feast proceeds, because a cousin might bring a friend or two, an aunt might bring a co-worker, or a next-door neighbor might smell the barbecue grilling and peek over the fence. They will be met with an invitation to come join the party. Early RSVPs don't matter for feasts. With our family feasts, we always say a mealtime prayer.

---

5. See Hunsinger's insight on Peter Martyr Vermigli's notion of transelementation and the Chalcedonian patterning of co-inherence, and the church's participation in the life of Christ (Hunsinger, *Eucharist and Ecumenism*, 355, 361).

6. See Cláudio Carvalhaes's extended treatment of the border-crossing, barrier-breaking power and orientation of the Eucharist (*Eucharist and Globalization*).

We give thanks to God for the gathering, for the provision of food, for family on both sides of the Pacific and all around the world. We pray for people without food and shelter. In this way, our feast is not solely about feeding those who are there. We are joined to every person in the world.

The nature of the joyful feast, the nature of the triune God, is to extend, to share, to give, to serve. Feasting is not about hoarding but about setting the table to bear witness to and express abundant joy and goodness; the table is set so all can come, all can partake, all can be fed.[7]

Let me return to that round eucharistic Table at Village Church that my colleague and I stood behind every month. Following the celebration of the eucharistic feast at Village Church is a closing hymn, and then the final pastoral charge and benediction. In fact, that round eucharistic Table is aligned with the center aisle, which leads out from the central sanctuary doors to the outdoor courtyard. Our going to the Table presupposes that from that Table—having been nourished, fed, strengthened, and reconnected to our risen and ascended Lord—the Spirit of Christ deploys us out into the world.

We somewhat mirror Jesus eating with his disciples at the beach barbecue he had with them as recounted in Luke 24:42. Jesus sends them out: "And they worshiped him, and returned to Jerusalem with great joy, and they were continually in the temple blessing God" (Luke 24:52). Jesus dines with his friends, and the text describes the scene: "While in their joy, they were disbelieving and still wondering" (Luke 24:41). The disciples are shocked at his appearing, their Teacher who they thought had died and is now in front of them.

Partaking in the joyful feast of God does not mean we have everything all figured out. The joyful feast of God does not mean that somehow our theology is all systematized, that we have life's ducks in a row, and that we are traversing life's pilgrimage with smiles and certainty. On the contrary, we are given the gifts of faith, hope, and love to propel us on the pilgrimage. These gifts keep us yearning for the invisible living God who encounters us and sustains us in ways both seen and unseen. God provides gifts with those whom we meet and in ways that the Spirit's work ministers to us. Joyful feast enables us to approach life and living with wonder, with curiosity, with contentment, with interest.

---

7. David Andrews asserts, "Eating is significant not only to personal behavior and individual actions; it is also related to a social order, to a food system." He continues: "Eating is a moral act. We are what we eat! And we can ask ourselves who is at the table? What are they saying about the food system?" ("Lord's Table," 70–71).

The joyful feast gives us love, what Mary Clark Moschella calls the "build effect" as a result of "broadening thought-action repertoires."[8] What Moschella describes is like a scaffold, as layer upon layer of interactions and conversations construct and broaden faith. It would be like the Lord's followers in every age, we are in joy while disbelieving and still wondering, even as the Lord is cooking up a feast of broiled fish for himself and for us hungry companions, all over the world. Where in one of his first appearances in Luke 24 he asks for food, in his third appearance with the disciples after the resurrection described in John 21:1–19, Jesus provides the food. It is Jesus who is preparing a fish fry, and the disciples are receiving confirmation of Jesus's identity after the resurrection. Each and every interaction and engagement with Jesus is this "build effect" of repertoires of faith, hope, love, and joy.

The round eucharistic Table at the sanctuary of Village Church reminds us of and prompts us to attend to unfinished business in the household of faith. Again Moschella's descriptor of "thought-action repertoires" is appropriate here. A "thought-action repertoire" of unfinished business sparked by the round eucharistic Table is the seemingly insurmountable matter of power, privilege, and authority. While the round eucharistic Table is meant to signal a universal welcome to all of God's children to feast at the Table that the Lord has prepared, we know from experience and from theological discourse that that does not reflect reality. It is difficult for many in the household of faith to rejoice when they are prevented from feasting at the Lord's Table if one is not Roman Catholic or Orthodox and such feasting occurs in the liturgical spaces of those particular ecclesial traditions. It is also difficult for many to rejoice when women and LGBTQIA+ siblings are prohibited from ever exercising liturgical leadership from behind the Table because of particular theologies that bar them from ecclesiastical ordination. And it is difficult to rejoice when particular ecclesial traditions insist as a nonnegotiable point of theology and authority that unless another ecclesial tradition has a polity of personal bishops, that absent ordination along the so-called apostolic succession through the episcopacy, then such ordained persons cannot exercise liturgical leadership from behind the Table.

I served as co-vice chair of the Third Round of Bilateral Dialogues between the Episcopal Church and the Presbyterian Church (U.S.A.) from 2019 to 2024. Building upon the progress of previous dialogues, both of our communions are preparing proposals for our respective national governing councils that allow a limited exchange of ministers to serve in one another's churches. If adopted and implemented, this proposal would be

---

8. Moschella, *Caring for Joy*, 43.

groundbreaking for our two denominations. For many years, our two denominations were stuck because the Episcopal Church did not recognize the ecclesial authority of pastors who were ordained by presbyteries and not a bishop in the apostolic succession. After many years, the Second Round of Bilateral Dialogues achieved a mutual recognition of ordained ministers, saying that on the basis of our common baptism, our vocational call to serve the people of God as church leaders can be affirmed by both churches. There was a further recognition that what is meant by *episkopē*, or the authority of bishop, does not exclusively mean an authority that is exercised by a single individual (bishop) but that such authority can be exercised by a council who has functioning authority of what a personal bishop would have. In the case of the Presbyterian Church (U.S.A.) polity, such authority is lodged in our presbyteries, or regional governing councils. The bilateral proposal coming to our respective national governing councils in the summer of 2024 marks a major step forward in not only mutual recognition of ordained ministries but the long-sought mutual reconciliation of ordained ministries. Approval of the proposal and its consequent implementation would go far in recognizing who is behind the Table, and would offer official legitimacy, authorization, and blessing that ecclesial power and liturgical privilege are in service to the community and to the wider mission of God in the church and in the world.

Our bilateral dialogue recognized that official church structures need to catch up with what God is and has been doing in the world. There are several Episcopal and Presbyterian ministries that are cooperating and exchanging ministers on the local level, particularly in campus ministries and congregations near college and university campuses where a theology of inclusive welcome is necessary to minister with and minister to young adults. The eucharistic Table—who is presiding, who is feasting, and who is absent from the feast—prompts us to examine what those theologies, ideologies, and assumptions are that stifle access to Joy. My close friend and pastor colleague, Kellen Smith, who serves as senior pastor and head of staff of the First Presbyterian Church in Wheaton, Illinois, took me on a tour of the church grounds when I was invited to be the guest preacher for their Distinguished Preacher series in 2018. His church was the first one that I have visited that has a eucharistic Table outside:

He says that they occasionally celebrate the Eucharist at that Table, particularly at Easter sunrise services. The Eucharist needs to be unlocked, both sacramentally and literally, from the confines of the church and oriented to God's presence and mission in the world.

Stained glass windows depicting scenes of Scripture face inward in the worshipping space for congregants inside to learn about the faith. Of course, the innovation of stained glass windows centuries ago occurred when congregants couldn't read, so like a comic strip, stained glass windows served the purpose of depicting the stories of our faith. Inward-facing stained glass windows also made congregants assured and nourished in the faith within the protective sanctuary of the church. That the Eucharist–Lord's Table–communion is also commonly located inside, it's no wonder that churches are regarded as insular, isolated, inward-facing communities. So whether visibly seeing the faith depicted on stained glass windows from the interior of the sanctuary, to tasting the faith from the Lord's Table within the interior confines of the church's sanctuary, what all this served was to make God's people feast among themselves for themselves. So much of American Christianity is reaping the fruits of a faith expressed in these architectural and liturgical embodiments that instill in the hearts and minds of God's people that the business of our faith is for *this* community, for the nourishment of those gathered here in *this* space.

And that there is what Joy is not. While it is certainly true that the Eucharist is a reassurance of God's promises in Christ for you and for me, it is not just for you and not just for me. I tell this to couples preparing to be married, families preparing for their child to be baptized, and loved ones preparing for the funeral of their loved ones—these events are in the context of the worship of God's people. Because these sacramental events occur in the context of a community and not as private ceremonies tucked away in a closet, this means, while it involves you or your loved one, it is not just about you or your loved one. This worship service is a public event and, therefore, blesses all of God's people gathered. It also blesses all of God's people scattered around the world. The event offers a witness of hope and joy to the world. In other words, whenever we gather, it is always in service to God for the life of the world.

So we minimize the Eucharist–Lord's Table–communion when we limit its celebration to the internal community of the church. In fencing the Table or in taking an ecclesial and ecclesiastical posture, whether explicitly or implicitly, that the activity of the Eucharist is just about us Christians who hold the union card for this church, we limit the theology of abundance that God intended for this sacrament. The Joy of God is lived out and embodied when the eucharistic life and witness is in the world, is for the world, is in solidarity with the world.

In the sixteenth century, when Calvin and his fellow Protestant Reformers were reforming liturgies, one aspect that Calvin retained of the medieval Mass and of ancient liturgies was that section of the eucharistic liturgy called the *Sursum Corda* (from the Latin, translated: "Lift up your hearts"). It is that part of celebrating the Eucharist when we as a community engage in the following dialogue:

Presider:	The Lord be with you.
Congregation:	And also with you.
Presider:	We lift up our hearts.
Congregation:	We lift them up to the Lord.
Presider:	Let us give thanks to the Lord our God.
Congregation:	It is right to give God thanks and praise.

There are variations on the verbiage, but that is the basic flow and content of the *Sursum Corda*. And while "Lift up your hearts" is one line, the whole dialogue is called *Sursum Corda*. Calvin and his contemporaries reacted against many parts of the medieval liturgy and accused the Church of Rome of liturgical accretions and abuse. But this section he retained and saw as pivotal to the meaning of the Eucharist–Lord's Table–communion.

Calvin emphasized the role, person, and efficacy of the Holy Spirit. The Spirit is the pivot and fulcrum of the Eucharist–Lord's Table–communion. Calvin and his Protestant contemporaries sought to make the case over and against the Church of Rome that partaking of the bread and wine at the eucharistic Table did not mean the literal eating of the literal body and blood of Christ. He argued that Eucharist–Lord's Table–communion did not mean the physical confinement of Christ who is already ascended in glory. Calvin saw that the Spirit was the lynchpin who made communion happen at Communion. Here are two sections of Calvin's *Institutes of the Christian Religion* that summarize this point:

> As we cannot at all doubt that it is bounded according to the invariable rule in the human body, and is contained in heaven, where it was once received, and will remain till it return to judgment, so we deem it altogether unlawful to bring it back under these corruptible elements, or to imagine it everywhere present. And, indeed, there is no need of this, in order to our partaking of it, since the Lord by his Spirit bestows upon us the blessing of being one with him in soul, body, and spirit. The bond of that connection, therefore, is the Spirit of Christ, who unites us to him, and is a kind of channel by which everything that Christ has and is, is derived to us. For if we see that the sun, in sending forth its rays upon the earth, to generate, cherish, and invigorate its offspring, in a manner transfuses its substance into it, why should the radiance of the Spirit be less in conveying to us the communion of his flesh and blood? Wherefore the Scripture, when it speaks of our participation with Christ, refers its whole efficacy to the Spirit.[9]

And then the work of Christ through the Spirit who transcends but who includes time and space:

> But if we are carried to heaven with our eyes and minds, that we may there behold Christ in the glory of his kingdom, as the symbols invite us to him in his integrity, so, under the symbol of bread, we must feed on his body, and, under the symbol of wine, drink separately of his blood, and thereby have the full enjoyment of him. For though he withdrew his flesh from us, and with his body ascended to heaven, he, however, sits at the right hand of the Father; that is, he reigns in power and majesty, and the glory of the Father. This kingdom is not limited by any intervals of space, nor circumscribed by any dimensions. Christ can exert his energy wherever he pleases, in earth and heaven, can manifest his presence by the exercise of his power, can always be present with his people, breathing into them his own life, can live in them, sustain, confirm, and invigorate them, and

---

9. Calvin, *Institutes*, 4.17.12.

preserve them safe, just as if he were with them in the body; in fine, can feed them with his own body, communion with which he transfuses into them. After this manner, the body and blood of Christ are exhibited to us in the sacrament.[10]

What we see here is how the Spirit of Christ, the fount of Joy and who is Joy itself, connects us with the Lord. In connecting us to Christ and keeping us united with Christ, the Spirit bestows upon us the benefits of Christ's own life, death, and resurrection. The Spirit also enables us to partake of Christ's ascended life in glory. Our communal partaking of the eucharistic Table of joy, then, is used by the Spirit to strengthen us and to energize us by virtue of this being the feast of God for the people of God. This is what the late Methodist liturgical historian, Laurence Stookey, called "Christ's Feast with the Church." The eucharistic event includes its elements, its location, its ritual performance, the presider, and the gathered assembly. They are not symbols on display or somehow conveying spiritual goods and services. The eucharistic event is a sacred arena where the Spirit of Christ is connecting us to Christ and to one another. At the same time, the Spirit of Christ is forming and shaping us to be agents of God's joy and justice in the world. Calvin's language is instructive on this point: "Christ can exert his energy wherever he pleases, in earth and heaven, can manifest his presence by the exercise of his power, can always be present with his people, breathing into them his own life, can live in them, sustain, confirm, and invigorate them, and preserve them safe." This is language of the Spirit—the Holy One who transcends time and space. The Spirit of Christ enables us to live in and with Christ in the world wherever we are. We live lives of thanksgiving, living in and with the One who is our Joy. This is to say, a life of joy is a life in which the living Joy is in communion with us by the Spirit of Joy. Thus, the power and promise of the Eucharist–Lord's Table–communion in both its sacramental and its missional dimensions are not to be confined to the internal life of the church. Rather the joyful feast is intended to be deployed. We are to bear witness to the action of God in the world. The eucharistic feast of joy is not to be hoarded, for God's blessings to be enjoyed for the sake of the participants. Rather, the feast is to recalibrate us for the witness in the world in which we reside.

The eucharistic feast of joy has much to do with remembering and being re-membered. When Jesus Christ instituted the feast, he said, "This is my body broken for you. Take, eat, do this in remembrance of me." Because we encounter numerous injustices, trials, forces, and factors that stifle joy in our lives, we often forget or neglect the love and joy of God. Thus, the eucharistic

---

10. Calvin, *Institutes*, 4.17.18.

promises of joy are given so that we may remember. But like tired and weary pilgrims on the journey, we also gather with the community of God's people to eat and drink. We gather to receive the gifts of God for the people of God. Our worn-out bodies and souls are being *re-membered*, being made whole again. We are put together again, so to speak, in order to live another day, in order to be bearers of Joy's light for another part of the journey.

Being with my extended family is about this act of remembering and sacred memory. I make it a point to travel to the Philippines once a year. Half of my two-week trip is teaching at Union Theological Seminary, to support and encourage my students, who are all pastors and community leaders. They serve in contexts of deep poverty, unclean sanitation, and political corruption. But they are a joy-filled and joyful people; they are part of my community as a Filipino American.

The other half of my trip is being with my grandparents. Before my paternal grandma was bedridden, she produced sumptuous Filipino food from her kitchen that no Michelin-star restaurant could match. Whether it be soups and stews and braised fish, complicated noodle dishes and sauces, or her famed mocha cake, Mama Pacing was a chef's chef in the kitchen. And she always prepared plenty for all to enjoy, enough for unexpected guests who might join for dinner. Her hospitality was expressed by both the quantity and the high quality of the food she prepared.

It was in that same kitchen where my grandma ran a side business for many years: a snack shop where, through a mosquito-screened door, school children could enter the back porch and see the various items for sale. She sold such things as bubble gum and candies, canned soda and chips. But the all-time favorite was her famous pickled papaya, which she made herself and packaged in sandwich bags with just enough pickling juice so that you could drink it to quench your thirst after a long day.

When I visit the Philippines, I think of my vigorous grandma and those bygone days. I remember the love embodied and expressed in that kitchen. I think of her in her housedress slicing and chopping, the sound of the mortar and pestle pressing the garlic and the other spices and herbs that would make ordinary chicken, beef, and fish an exquisite feast for the palette. I look back on those memories in my visits to the Philippines not so much with nostalgia, but more with deep thanksgiving. When I see my frail grandma in bed or in her wheelchair being attended to by her caregivers, I see one who exuded the joy and love of God, who helped raise me, whose quarters and dimes and dollar bills earned from that snack store helped to buy me my first car and helped to pay for my college apartment through my undergraduate years.

My grandpa is no longer with us, having succumbed to the adverse effects of COVID-19, but his faith and love lives on. I timed my last visit to the Philippines to coincide with my grandpa's birthday, and I was there with him before COVID-19 struck the world in 2020. He wanted a watch, so before I left, I went to a jewelry store and bought him one. The last photo I have with him shows Grandpa Ensoy wearing his birthday watch on his outdoor rocking chair, smiling from ear to ear. As his body was failing due to COVID, one of his caregivers FaceTimed our family so that we could say our goodbyes and offer prayers. I led the prayer time, offering him a blessing and giving thanks to God for his life. He was wearing that birthday watch as he lay there dying. He couldn't speak. I don't know if he heard our voices through the caregiver's phone. Months after his death my aunt visited and brought back that watch, which I keep as a way of remembering. These past few years since his death when I visit the Philippines, I go back to the family feast, to my Grandma Pacing's kitchen, and to the faith we share.

I am reminded that we confess that part of the Apostles' Creed on the "communion of saints" in the paragraph that starts with "I believe in the Holy Spirit." I was baptized in the Roman Catholic Church. When I exercised my faith in Protestant churches as a young adult, I did not fully appreciate nor understand why a large swath of Christians venerate saints or offer prayers through saints. Years later, I understand and appreciate the practice and theology behind it. It wasn't just theological reflection or PhD work in liturgical studies; it was the lived faith of my grandparents that brought me to an appreciation of this practice. My paternal grandparents were conservative Catholics. My paternal grandma had a painting and a statue of Mary, the mother of Jesus, outside of her bedroom. At their house in Guam, Mother Mary cradling the infant Jesus is encased in glass. The Holy Spirit connects us to the physical living and the physical dead in some mysterious, sacramental way. There was a common practice once upon a time that, following a special feast day or on the week of a deceased's birthday, parishioners would go to the burial site of departed loved ones and hold an agape love feast there so as to celebrate the life of the deceased. This act of communion with loved ones came from the belief that we are in communion with those whom we loved and who love us still. Remembering and being re-membered are matters of being in communion with loved ones, with neighbors, with strangers, and indeed with all of God's people in every time and in every place. It is the faith and love and joy of my grandparents—and their legacies which live on—that enable me to minister, and to serve as best as I can by God's abundant grace.

Joy's feast, as expressed in family feasts and in memories of the feasts my grandma prepared, connects us to the ancestors. I appreciate the robust notion of prayer that understands death as a return to the realm of the ancestors, who welcome us to the heavenly family. Whenever we feast and eat and pray, we do so with the understanding that we are feasting and worshipping with the ancestors of the family and of faith. When I learn to cook a Filipino dish, I see that as preparing a recipe passed down from generations, partaking in a rich practice of my ancestors. Whenever an African, African American, or Caribbean friend or colleague experiences the death of a loved one, they customarily say something to the effect of, "He has gone home to the ancestors. May he rise in power and glory." Death is seen as a homegoing, where the ancestors, the communion of the saints, await. Such a depth of faith is the work of the Spirit who comforts our mourning with the resounding assurance of joy. It's being re-membered through the Spirit of Joy who mends us, who invigorates us, who heals us, who turns our mourning in the night to dancing in the morning.

As a minister and pastor theologian who is Filipino Pacific Islander American, I understand my vocation for justice in church, academy, and society as being a part of the struggle of the ancestors. Notice I said "the ancestors" and not just "my ancestors." The ancestors of the faith are the communion of saints. I belong to the wider ancestry, the communion, in a long train of those who have gone before me and who will continue after I join that eternal communion. As with us who are still living in body and flesh, theirs was a journey for justice, reconciliation, and all those human engagements that make life worth living. Lives lived in joy give purpose to human existence, committed in service to others so that all may flourish.

Joy's call and commitment are for justice in church and society. Such a call means that all are welcome. This means those in the pew, those in pulpits and behind the Lord's Table, are all welcome. In other words, clergy and congregants, and indeed all who are baptized in Christ, are welcome at Joy's feast. The Lord's feast Table, Christ's banquet of joy, is for all to receive and share in the One who is our Joy.

The work and struggle for a justice that welcomes all people are long. The work of justice that seeks for all to be fed, for all to be a part of co-creating their futures at decision-making tables, is a long struggle. The struggle for justice in church and society is one where we pray and hope for a day where all can say "Amen" and "Thanks be to God." The journey is hard, with treacherous paths, and we will hunger for justice when it seems like an insurmountable and impossible goal.

But we are nourished on the journey by the living Christ, who feeds us and sustains us for that work and witness in the world. The Lord does this, not just for our sake, but for the life of the world. The Lord's heart of joy was to serve, to give, to love. His life and his heart are what pattern our own life's purpose and goal. In this fuller way, our lives are eucharistic when the mind and heart of Christ are inscribed upon us by the Spirit. In this way, our lives, and this world, are sacred tables where God is transforming the ordinary into something extraordinary beyond our thinking and imagination.

FOR REFLECTION

1. The late Methodist liturgy scholar Laurence Hull Stookey called the Eucharist "Christ's Feast with the Church." In what ways is giving thanks always a communal act?
2. For whom and for what do you give thanks?
3. How might fellowship at tables and fellowship at the Table be a joyful feast for all? What are obstacles or threats to table fellowship being joyful, being feasts, and being "for all"?
4. Who are missing at your table/the Lord's Table celebrations?

PRAYER

Bread of Life, Cup of Salvation, you are the Lord Christ, who gave your life for the life of the world. You nourish us and sustain us for life's journey, you unite us to yourself and strengthen us so that we might bear witness of your love, serving others, reconciling others to yourself. Make our feasting joyful, encountering you at the center and circumference of every table and at your own Table, for all those places belong to you. Help us welcome neighbors and strangers in our midst, that all may be fed and nourished by what you provide. Fill us with joy, your joy, your Spirit who is our everlasting Joy. We give you thanks. Amen.

5

JOY'S WORK AND WITNESS

I can't breathe...
—George Floyd

Christ's love moves the world to reconciliation and unity.
—Theme of the Eleventh Assembly of the World Council of Churches (2022)

Go where you must go, and hope!
—Gandalf, in J. R. R. Tolkien, *The Lord of the Rings*

Joy has a mission. Joy is on a mission.

The ordered worship service is completed with the presiding minister pronouncing a benediction, a good word. In all the benedictions I offered when I served for eight years on the pastoral staff of Village Community Presbyterian Church in Rancho Santa Fe, California, I always raised my right hand with the ancient gesture depicted in many icons and mosaics. The gesture consists of the thumb and ring finger of the right hand pressed together with the index finger and pinky finger slightly raised and the middle finger slightly curved. The placement of the fingers spelled the Greek letters of the Lord's name, as well as depicted the truth of the Trinitarian Godhead and the two natures of Jesus Christ subsisting in One person.

All of that theology in one gesture as the Aaronic blessing "the Lord bless you and keep you" (Num 6:24–26) or the Pauline blessing "now to God who is able" (Eph 3:20–21) was proclaimed. This blessing—both in gesture and by proclaimed words—is offered after the gathered people of God have sung hymns, psalms, and spiritual songs. The benediction is gifted after the people of God have offered their own prayers, read and meditated upon Scripture, heard and received a sermon/homily preached from the pulpit, partaken of the sacramental body and blood of Christ, and perhaps renewed the baptismal covenant. Following all of this, the people of God expect to depart, ready to face their lives, and begin another week. For some, it's a welcome end to a long service, as some look forward to the conversation and catching up on the past week's happenings; in Christian circles we call this "fellowship" or "sharing prayer concerns."

But here, as the doors are flung open and the noontime daylight enters the sanctuary and parishioners exit, some head to brunch, others will tee off at the golf course, others will pick up their children from Sunday school and head to a sporting event. Still others will look forward to a small group gathering, join a church meeting, or find a wooden bench under a tree and reflect upon what just happened in the worship service. There are others who live alone and who crack a smile but whose eyes reveal a deep loneliness. The boisterous worship service will turn to the silence of their house.

Regardless of how parishioners spend the rest of their Sunday, they must face Monday morning soon after. Then what? What do we do with the cosmic claims and cosmological promises that we have entrusted our lives and this world? Joy has a hold on us because we are created to "glorify God and enjoy Him forever." With the avalanche of life that comes our way, including many noble and noteworthy aims that compete for our time and attention, we are called by the One who is our joy to live the life for which God sent Christ to give his life "for the life of the world," as the late Orthodox liturgist Alexander Schmemann says. That is, being in communion with Christ means that, "nevertheless I live, yet not I, but Christ lives in me. And the life I live, I live by the faith of the Son of God, who loved me and gave himself for me" (Gal 2:20). Christ's life was for the life of the world. Christ's life was for reconciling the world to God's self, to right the wrongs that we find in our common humanity. Christ's life was committed to restoring the brokenness in the shalom vision of transformative justice where all can flourish, where all are well; that is the divine agenda. This is the Trinitarian mission and vision. This becomes our agenda as ones who have been redeemed by that same God.

The aim of our experiencing joy—that is, of living in the heart and life of God—is not for the existential, phenomenological ecstasy of feeling good. We are not created as if God's work of reconciliation on Christ's cross and at the empty tomb were cheapened to personal fulfillment or personal nirvana. Such self-hoarding would put to waste the wider significance of Christ's mission and the God-given freedom we have been given. Mathewes describes the "radical existential turbulence" of this paradox that we have in seeking joy because joy is a "fugitive."[1] We pursue joy but never catch it because it is in the "middle voice."[2] We both act on it and receive it, an immanence and a transcendence. So when we are caught in joy, we are surrounded by cultural signals, "society's basic energy . . . that constantly undermines, directly and indirectly, the stability and commitment to long-term aims that has been the fundament of moral formation in traditional societies."[3] So here's where the worship of God puts the aperture of joy in proper perspective. Moltmann asserts:

> Where repentance is understood as a spiritual return to the evil and rejected past, it deals in self-accusation, contrition, sackcloth and ashes. But repentance is a return to the future, it becomes concrete in rejoicing, in new self-confidence and in love.[4]

He continues:

> But if repentance as return to the future already is rejoicing in freedom, then out of that joy it should also be possible to bring about changes of unjust and oppressive social and political conditions.[5]

What joy does, when connected to our worship of the One who is our joy, is direct us towards tomorrow. Joy points us to God's future, as ones who have been freed to love God. Joy connects us to love neighbor and stranger, to clothe the naked, to feed the hungry, to proclaim freedom to the captive, to care for the orphans and widows, to "do justice, love mercy, and walk humbly with our God" (Mic 6:8).

Joy is living in the heart and life of God. The living God—the One revealed as Father, Son, and Holy Spirit—acts out of love because the triune God is love itself (1 John 4:16). The triune God is the preeminent embodiment and enactment of love. This means, then, that the God of justice, in righting the wrongs of the world, does so out of love; justice and love go hand in hand. God's righteousness flows from God's nature and character of

1. Mathewes, "Toward Theology of Joy," 77, 89.
2. Mathewes, "Toward Theology of Joy," 66.
3. Mathewes, "Toward Theology of Joy," 77.
4. Moltmann, *Theology of Joy*, 63.
5. Moltmann, *Theology of Joy*, 64.

love. When a human being who has been trafficked is set free and her perpetrator/victimizer is brought to justice, the restorative justice is God's act of love to begin to heal the brokenness of humanity's violence. Restorative justice is to be in solidarity with both sets of human beings torn asunder, marred by the ugly and pervasive destruction of sin's grip on the human heart. God who is Justice, God who is Joy, God who is Love communes with us, brings us into the triune community.

This is what liturgical theologian David Fagerberg calls "liturgical mysticism."[6] The triune God, through the ministry of Word and sacrament, inscribes upon our hearts the divine mission, vision, and values. The triune God strengthens and enables our lives to follow the pattern of God.

The Confession of 1967 in the Presbyterian Reformed theological tradition has this powerful description of our life's template:

> The life, death, resurrection, and promised coming of Jesus Christ has set the pattern for the church's mission. His human life involves the church in the common life of all people. His service to men and women commits the church to work for every form of human well-being. His suffering makes the church sensitive to all human suffering so that it sees the face of Christ in the faces of persons in every kind of need. His crucifixion discloses to the church God's judgment on the inhumanity that marks human relations and the awful consequences of the church's own complicity in injustice. In the power of the risen Christ and the hope of his coming, the church sees the promise of God's renewal of human life in society and of God's victory over all wrong.[7]

Divine joy imprints and encodes upon our hearts as Christ's church the joyful, joy-filled obligation, commitment, and calling to follow the ways of our Lord, whose very life and mission was a joy and delight to his heavenly Father, to our Father in heaven. This tells us much about what joy's consequence and outcome are in our lives. Let's put it in human terms that our human nature and that our culture will understand: Do you want to feel and be in joy, to *en*-joy life to the fullest? Then live the life of Christ, who is our Joy.

And what is that life? It's a life marked by service for the reconciliation of the world, which engages in prayerful action and active prayer for

---

6. Fagerberg puts it aptly: "Liturgical mysticism is becoming by grace what Christ is by nature" (*Liturgical Mysticism*, 52). More densely but with textual depth he asserts that liturgical mysticism is "the Paschal mystery hypostasizing in our hearts. Liturgy's business is to celebrate the Paschal mystery, and when it does, the mystery hypostasizes in us, descends to us, takes up its home in us, becomes the substances of our lives" (78).

7. Office of the General Assembly, *Book of Confessions*, §9.32, 292.

God's shalom vision of transformative justice to be effected in the world. God is passionate for the world that the Lord created. God is so in love for the creation and every creature. That is why God's own Word resounds the praises of the creation and creatures back to our Creator; Psalms 145–50 are a crescendo fortissimo summoning everyone, everything, "all that has breath" to be free to praise God.

Because of the oppressive nature of sin, in its personal forms, its communal dimensions, its systemic features, its historical perpetuation, and its generational effects, God's work of transformative justice calls forth the Lord's redeemed to be vigilant against powers and principalities. Empowered by joy, God's children confront all that seek to frustrate God's love, all that contradict and contravene God's Joy for the Lord's creation and for God's creatures. The work of justice, as Jesus himself encountered barriers and blockages throughout his ministry with the disciples, is a long struggle; *la lucha* (Spanish for struggle), *pakikibaka* (Tagalog for struggle) is arduous. The struggle for God's justice requires resilience as it is taxing on the body. The journey for justice wearies the mind. The pilgrimage for justice crushes the spirit. It calls forth every part of our being when we are serious about what it means, when what is at stake is the flourishing of all of God's people.

When George Floyd was murdered by police officers as he cried out "I can't breathe" twenty-eight times for eight minutes and forty-six seconds with an officer's knee on his neck and back, his struggle captured the world's attention. But more than that, he gave voice to Black communities everywhere as they had experienced and continue to experience the crushing effects of unjust laws and unequal application of laws and practices on whole communities and neighborhoods. From enslavement, to lynching, to housing and lending practices that perpetuated poverty, to unequal distribution of funding and unequal access to healthcare and economic and educational opportunities, the "I can't breathe" succinctly uttered the struggle of Black bodies under the literal weight of the state.

When my eldest son and I decided to join a peaceful demonstration in downtown San Diego in the summer 2020, we carefully prepared our placard that read "I can't breathe," calling for justice for Floyd. On the car ride downtown, my son, who had just turned seventeen years old and who would be in college a year later, asked, "I want to do more. What more can I do? I feel frustrated that I can't do more." I internalized his words and his question, for his generation, the Google generation or the so-called Gen Z, was born in a world where digital images, the data revolution, and mobile devices were the mainstays of communication and community. It was through the instantaneous volume and velocity of those media that he and billions of others became conscientized about the brokenness of this world.

They were already aware of the massive scale of the hurt of planet Earth. The death struggle of this one man named George Floyd voiced the struggle of his ancestors, of his family, of his community. In a deep way, he was giving voice to my son and his generation. I told Daniel that he was already doing something by going to this rally. I said that he had a responsibility as a Filipino Korean American to learn about his heritage and to conscientize his White friends where they are color blind. I shared with him how it was important for him as a soon-to-be college student to learn more and become more knowledgeable. I added that in each season of his life he will be given opportunities to speak and to act, and that as he grows in stature and as his realm of responsibilities are expanded through a professional career or his future vocation, his sphere of influence will widen and he will be called to partake of the struggle in different ways. As a student, there will be ways, such as the street demonstration, that he can do with other peers that don't necessarily require particular resources. If he were to be an attorney in the future, I said, or a diplomat in the US Foreign Service, those arenas would enable him to engage in the struggle for justice in other ways. For now, as a student, he has some meaningful ways to engage, although they may feel limited. He also has a responsibility to learn as much as he can about history, religions, philosophy, and other disciplines to hone his mind and heart for what God may call him to be and to become.

When we arrived at the student demonstration in front of the county administration building, there were several hundred adolescents and college-aged people calling for justice for George Floyd and reforms for police training and use of force. It was a peaceful demonstration. Then the police helicopters hovered overhead and tear-gas cannisters were launched into the crowd. We dispersed with the crowd, trying to cover our eyes and mouth, but some vapors made it into our eyes, and we were brought to tears. We could see some people carrying jugs of milk, dousing their eyes. We managed to run to our car and collect ourselves. In the succeeding weeks I participated in Zoom webinars with other community groups and advocacy leaders calling for police reforms and enhanced community relations. It took several months, but the San Diego City Council and Police Department agreed upon modified policies and guidelines for use of force, the use of de-escalation methods, and the establishment of a community relations board with broadened powers to follow through on citizen concerns and to cultivate stronger ties between the police and the communities in which they serve.

At about the same time as those events that summer, I participated in the planning team for a solidarity prayer vigil between Black and Asian American faith leaders that was planned for the Crenshaw neighborhood of south-central Los Angeles at Leimert Park Village Plaza. Dubbed "AAPI (Asian American Pacific Islander) Christians for Black Lives: A Vigil of Love and Solidarity," the gathering was a public witness of racial reconciliation between two communities—Black and AAPI—that historically have been in conflict with one another, including in the 1990s. In the riots following the police beating of the unarmed Black motorist Rodney King in Los Angeles, which fueled the anger of Black communities in south-central Los Angeles, there was significant looting and destruction of many Asian-owned businesses and residences. We who are leaders in AAPI and Black faith communities wanted to write a different narrative and carve out a different trajectory. It was critical that we pray together, that we express our solidarity in our shared faith in Christ and in our common cause for racial justice, healing, and advocacy.

While summer 2020 had been the time planned for Daniel and me to use a Louisville Institute Pastoral Study Grant to hike the Camino de Santiago, the onset of COVID-19, coupled with the work for racial justice, delayed our pilgrimage. I see God's providence in that delay. Had we gone that summer, this project would not have had the texture of justice linked with joy linked with worship as it has now. COVID-19 put in the forefront the stark, long-standing reality of racial injustice in the United States, as experienced, for example, within my own community of Filipino Americans. Many Filipino Americans are employed in the healthcare industry as nurses and doctors, as well as in the US Postal Service. COVID-19 was not a time for rest nor for quarantine for many Filipino Americans as they had an obligation to work and care for others, but in doing so they endangered themselves and their families. Before COVID-19, I teamed up with a group of Filipino American scholars from the American Academy of Religion to secure funding from the Louisville Institute for a Collaborative Inquiry Team grant to explore Filipino American theologies. As COVID-19 hit, we became interested in analyzing the effects of COVID-19—how Filipino Americans engaged their faith and how community was formed and strengthened in this period of both a health pandemic and the endemic of racial injustice. The spiritual, psychological, physiological, and emotional toll that COVID-19 took on us researchers was such that we had many Zoom sessions where we just cried with one another, took time to reflect upon the rising death tolls, and encouraged one another during the unmitigated racial strife spurned on by former US President Donald Trump and the January 6 insurrection.

Our group of six scholars found a community among ourselves, and in doing so, discovered that that shared struggle to survive the pandemic and endemic was the very method of our Filipino American community in diaspora. That is, what enables Filipinos on both sides of the Pacific to live and thrive with vibrant faith is what is called, in Tagalog, *kapwa*.

In its fullness and richness, *kapwa* is unity in and for the community, a view of the self in relation to the whole village (the *barangay*), the whole family, the whole nation, and, indeed, all of creation. *Kapwa* enables one to find strength, purpose, and meaning in the wider community to which we belong and are therefore responsible for the well-being of all. It is both a gift and a calling to hold *kapwa* in one's heart; it is ingrained in the Filipino heart and soul as it keeps us connected one to another, looking out for each other, and seeing to it that we lift one another up so that all rejoice, or all grieve, or all celebrate. Our *kapwa*, as we were dispersed across the United States, kept us not only sane, but also grounded in our humanity. We strived to survive the COVID-19 pandemic and the endemic of racism. But we sought and prayed not just to survive, but to come out whole in our being. We hoped that we would come out stronger, ready to fight the good fight. We were determined, in our relative young ages and at early points in our respective academic careers, that we had plenty more to write and publish, we had many more sermons and lectures to offer, we had many more platforms to advocate from. We were resilient in our determination because we had many more organizations to participate in, organize, and lead; we had many more rallies to attend; we had many more fliers to print, many more generations to inspire, equip, and support. We understood—and we still understand—our pilgrimage as a sacred call for justice. We understand our vocation as a sacred call from God, one marked with joy and with love for God, for one another, for our *kababayan* (fellow Filipinos), and for our shared humanity.

I lost my paternal grandfather in the Philippines to COVID-19. My Papa Ensoy (Lorenzo Dayday Presa) was ninety-two years old. In spring 2024, we lost my paternal grandma, Mama Pacing. Before the pandemic, I made it a point to travel regularly to the Philippines during August to visit my paternal grandparents and to teach at Union Theological Seminary in Dasmariñas, Cavite, which is about an hour-long drive from my grandparents' home.

Union Seminary is a school founded by Presbyterians, Congregationalists, and Methodists, and has trained many church leaders since its founding in 1907. Known as the "School of the Prophets," Union Seminary has historically been and continues to be on the vanguard of advocacy for the marginalized, speaking truth to power, understanding its holy vocation to be about God's transformative justice. The seminary's Salakot Chapel is a round structure whose doors are often open during community worship, keeping the breeze flowing in an otherwise temperate climate. Gathered in that space with my *kababayan* and looking outside with the trees swaying and the sunlight shining, I see and feel the power of the Holy Spirit breathing life in our community, anchoring me to who I am, filling me with such exuberant joy of being among prophets and prophetesses for the holy vocation of justice. In a land rife with political corruption that forces Filipinos to remain in abject poverty, where the aristocracy collude with political elites to increase their wealth at the expense of millions of the Philippines' poor, the seminary is a hub of joy. Here in the seminary and in every church I visit—Roman Catholic and Protestant alike—the faith is vibrant, joy filled, and joyful. Hospitality abounds; generosity grounded in *kapwa* means no one is turned away but all are welcome and considered as family (as *tita* [aunt], *tito* [uncle], *kuya* [older brother], *ate* [older sister; pronounced ah-teh], *lola* [grandmother], *lolo* [grandfather]). Whatever age one may be, they are given that term of endearment as a member of the extended family. It's *kapwa* for *pakikibaka*. That is, we are community for the sake of the struggle for justice.[8] We are together not just for the sake of being together. Rather, we are together as both a sign of justice (against forces and factors that would tear us apart or keep us divided) and as agents and co-conspirators for justice (committing ourselves through holy worship to be strengthened and lead by the Spirit of God to work for God's transformative justice). Because most Filipinos and Filipino Americans in the diaspora are Christians—Roman Catholic and Protestant—we live our lives, raise our families, and enter our vocations with faith as guide, purpose, framework, and anchor.

My *kababayan* in the Philippines, including my students and faculty colleagues at Union Seminary, are committed to God's transformative justice. The indigenous theology in the Philippines is called the "theology of struggle," locating the struggle in Christ's suffering on the cross and understanding that Christ is in solidarity with the Filipino people. For we on this side of the Pacific, children and grandchildren and great-grandchildren of the diaspora, ours is a commitment to transformative justice as a response to God's providence that brought us here. God enables us to live with the opportunities afforded to us by way of our geographical location, but the commitment and responsibility to justice are the same, if not greater. Our worship of God reminds us of that calling, that we are less than Filipino, we are less than human, frankly, if we are not working towards the betterment of all. Thus, we are not joyful, joy filled, and living out joy when we are not about God's transformative justice. Otherwise, what good was the sacrifice

---

8. For a more extensive analysis of the relationship of *kapwa* and *pakikibaka*, see Presa, *Ascension Theology and Habakkuk*.

of my great-grandparents, and my grandparents after them, and my parents after them if I were to hoard my education and vocational accomplishments just to myself or for reputation and accolades? All those things are for nothing if the goal were not to participate in God's mission of reconciliation, justice, the healing of the nations, and the shalom of all of God's creation.

We are fully alive, and therefore in joy and *en*-joying life, when we are in the heart and life of God. This means being attuned to the mission, vision, and values of the living God, as revealed in Jesus Christ, in the unity and fellowship of the Holy Spirit. We are more fully human when we embody the life pattern of Christ's own life. The pattern of Christ's own life was one marked by service to reconcile all of God's people to himself. That's what brought him greatest joy, when he was connected to the mission of his and our heavenly Father. When tasks, causes, projects, callings, priorities, schedules, appointments, or responsibilities become ends in themselves, no matter how good or noble they may be, unmoored from their essence of being acts of worship to the living God, those things become just that: things. Another thing to do. Another family responsibility. They either become a burden, or they become ends in themselves and therefore hoarded for their own good rather than connected to the wider and deeper intention of God to cultivate hearts, lives, and communities where the shalom vision of transformative justice is inculcated. We will miss the sacred domains and arenas of God's joy where the wider purpose of reconciliation of all of creation and all of humanity occur. That is when we know and can recognize and experience the fullness of joy, the advent of Joy, living in the One who is our Joy.

The work and witness of joy in our daily life, in every facet of our life, for all of our life are holding to the sacred vocation that the entirety of our living existence is worship. We are called "to present our bodies as a living sacrifice, holy and acceptable to God, which is your spiritual worship" (Rom 12:1). I appreciate that the work and witness of joy happen in real time, in the wild and crazy of the lives we live. This is not a utopian illusion where all is perfect and where we bask in endless, flawless joy.

On my Spotify playlist is an eclectic selection. I have such artists as Dua Lipa, Coldplay, and James Ingram, together with Rihanna and Calvin Harris, the sacred tunes of Taizé, the soul music of Aretha Franklin, and the classical compositions of Vivaldi. One afternoon, I was running errands and listening to the song "Goodness of God," performed by Jenn Johnson.[9] At the moment I sang the part of the lyrics that proclaim that I will sing about the goodness of God, all of a sudden there was a driver who cut me off. My

---

9. "Goodness of God," by Ben Fielding et al., featuring Bethel Music and Jenn Johnson, on *Victory (Live)*, Capitol CMG Paragon 2018.

next breath was an expletive, and after the rude motorist had passed and I looked at his vehicle with stinging eyes, I ironically continued singing the part of the song that describes our singing as breath. I laughed in my car at that expression of true humanity. Living in and with the joy of God is not having a halo above our heads while we consistently follow the guidance of the angel perched on our right shoulders. Rather, it's living in the healthy tension of being aware of the goodness of God and the presence of God even as we're being cut off by a driver. In fact, it's a quite healthy response to express that frustration, not in the violent way of ramming my vehicle into his car, but rather to express my anger in a safe space and in a productive way rather than bottling it up in my spirit.

We see the work and witness of joy as a way of being and doing when our faith holds the cross and resurrection as concurrent realities rather than as a linear progression. During his ministry, Jesus was continually aware of the shadow of death that lingered. He was also aware of the divine promise of renewed life, of resurrection power. His life was holding those promises concurrently in his one person.

We behold the work and witness of joy in the paradoxes and seeming contradictions of our human experiences. It was the week before Holy Week this past spring 2024 when I received the news that my paternal grandma had died in the Philippines after a bout with pneumonia. I had said my goodbye to her on my last visit to the Philippines two years prior, but it wasn't until the reality of her death that it hit me: Mama Pacing is gone. Within minutes of receiving that news, I also learned that I had been offered a ministry opportunity that I had been awaiting. It was holding both pieces of news in tension, gazing out my hotel room, beholding the sky's hues at sunset, that I felt both sadness and joy, loss and gain, emptiness and satisfaction. It was a weird feeling, neither at Good Friday's cross nor at Easter's resurrection. It was like being in Saturday's tomb where Christ's body lay, in the darkness and quiet where there was no movement. It was a zero-sum feeling, to put it in accounting terms.

When we arrived in the Philippines a few days later for my Mama Pacing's funeral, it wasn't a somber occasion, but rather one filled with celebration. There was feasting, sharing family stories, and faith with daily Mass and prayers. What was remarkable about a Filipino funeral, which I had never experienced in all my years as either attendee or officiant at funerals in the United States, was that in our family village (*barangay*), there was a twenty-four-hour vigil for a whole week as family members, friends of our family, and our household staff took turns watching my grandma's body in the mortuary chapel. On the day of her funeral, the vigils ended and her coffin was placed in a hearse. Leading the hearse to the *barangay* church a mile away was a forty-member marching band. Behind the hearse was our extended family, and behind us were friends and citizens of the *barangay*. It was a one-mile pilgrimage as we walked at a slow pace through the main street of the *barangay*, with all traffic stopped, residents and shopkeepers watching us, some pedestrians joining us, and others throwing coins on the ground to wish us luck and show support. It was a pilgrimage of faith as we passed by road signs that I had driven by for many years and now saw up close, as each sign pointed to other parts of the Philippines. This took back my memory to three years earlier when Daniel and I were on the Camino de Santiago. This pilgrimage in the Philippines was to consecrate and commit my last grandparent into the arms and heart of God.

Following Mass, where I shared a eulogy about Mama Pacing, our family and the townspeople repeated the pilgrimage and accompanied Mama Pacing's coffin back to the mortuary a mile away. This time, her return to the mortuary was to the specially constructed family mausoleum where my paternal grandpa's, Papa Ensoy's, cremains were held. My family asked me to do the sacred honor of offering the prayer of committal as Papa Ensoy's cremains, contained in an urn, were carefully placed in Mama Pacing's coffin, signifying their reunion. I offered a prayer, committing both of my grandparents to God's heart, holding onto the promise of resurrection glory, even as we are joined to them through the Holy Spirit and in every table where we share the faith and share family stories. Minutes after I offered that consecratory prayer of dedication, my grandparents' remains were both placed into the mausoleum and it was sealed. There they were laid to rest. Their pain and struggles were gone. Their baptisms were complete. Between them they spent almost two centuries of life on this earth, raising a family, working to earn a living, supporting me through college and seeing me graduate, dedicating their lives to the Lord through weekly Mass and daily prayers of the Lord's Prayer—their pilgrimages had come to an end, and they had commenced an everlasting delight within the realm of the ancestors in the presence of the Living Joy.

Pilgrimages are sacred because the Living Joy makes an appearance when you don't expect. The day after Mama Pacing's funeral was Palm Sunday. Our family drove to Tagaytay to attend worship at the chapel of Munting Bukal (Little Springs), a pilgrimage site founded by our Auntie Lily Manalo near the Pink Sisters convent of the Missionaries of Charity. The provincial Catholic bishop who officiated at Mama Pacing's funeral the day prior was the Palm Sunday preacher. But it was Auntie Lily's message to us after the service that was the Word of God for the people of God. Following the Palm Sunday service, we joined worshippers for a traditional Filipino breakfast of *champorado* (chocolate rice), *dilis* (salted fish), *pan de sal* (bread roll), *queso* (cheese), *buchi* (sesame ball filled with red bean paste), and *ube halaya* (purple yam jam).

This breakfast prepared by the convent nuns filled our bodies and hearts with love and joy. The Living Joy was making the Spirit's presence known. Auntie Lily, a nonagenarian who exudes a humble gravitas with her gentle piercing eyes, silver hair, and dignified voice, embodies a robust faith. Her deep wisdom is forged from a life that experienced travails and toils, of which her mangled left hand was the visible evidence and to which her life's story bore witness.

I share her testimony to you with her blessing and permission, although she was one who hesitated at first as she is not one to seek attention or praise. Our family literally sat at her feet with the provincial bishop sitting at an adjacent bench as Auntie Lily began to testify about her mangled hand. She told how when she was seven years old, during the Second World War, her father brought home an unexploded grenade. Like any child, she was curious about what he found, and so he gave it to her, thinking that it no longer contained any danger. Little did either of them know that the grenade was very much live; she almost lost her life as her hand was reduced to hanging skin, mangled bones, and blood everywhere. Her father was distraught all his life, feeling the weight of guilt. But Auntie Lily kept close to her dad, reassuring him that it wasn't his fault and that she loved him dearly. Years later, when her parents died, Auntie Lily used the family inheritance to donate the land to the Missionaries of Charity to establish Munting Bukal (Little Springs), also called Munting Kanlungan (Little Shade). Her calling was to establish a place where the downtrodden, the downcast, the forgotten, and all of God's children who need a safe refuge for healing and wholeness could come without judgment. Auntie Lily shared that over the many decades that Munting Bukal has been serving countless strangers who literally appear at their doorsteps, she has met face to face with drug addicts, sex addicts, drug dealers, murderers, thieves, and alcoholics, among many others. She told the story of a businessman who cancelled his trip to Switzerland because he had heard of Munting Bukal and was eager to meet with Auntie Lily and get his heart and mind in the right place. He hopped over the fence of the pilgrimage refuge site and spent a few days with Auntie Lily and the Missionaries of Charity community. She has been asked by loved ones if she ever fears for her own safety as this stranger, like many strangers, came to Munting Bukal when she didn't know anything about him. She said she is not fearful because she knows that God intends for those strangers to come to Munting Bukal and that she is grateful and blessed that this "Little Spring" is a "Little Shade" for all of God's children and is being put to the use that God intended.

In sharing this testimony, Auntie Lily concluded with these nuggets of wisdom to our family and to the listening bishop. With her mangled hand, she pointed to the circle gathering around her and said, "Our time here will not be repeated. This is a sacred time. This is a sacrament. This is the sacrament of presence." She went on to say, "Be present. I have learned to be present. When you are fully present, you will know the presence of God." She concluded with this insight gleaned from her years of reflection and meditation, not in isolation but in the daily engagement with the Living Joy and with the lives of God's children: "Just as the sun rises and sets each day, God likes simplicity." She said to love and to forgive and to welcome are not difficult, but pretty simple and straightforward. You are just to love, to forgive, to welcome. Hers is a life that follows the Living Joy in simply welcoming all so that all of God's beloved children may experience plain joy, generous love, and a shade of peace for the journey.

The writer of the New Testament book of Hebrews exhorted followers of Christ to "continually offer a sacrifice of praise to God" (Heb 13:15) and connected our living worship with doing good and sharing what we have (Heb 13:16).

A common pastoral charge and benediction to conclude worship services is this:

> Go out into the world in peace; have courage; hold onto what is good; return no one evil for evil; strengthen the fainthearted; support the weak and help the suffering; honor all people; love and serve the Lord, rejoicing in the power of the Holy Spirit.[10]

In the Latin Mass, the benediction is named *Ite, Missa est*, which literally means "Go, it has been sent," or more colloquially translated, "Go, you are sent" or "Go, you are dismissed." Taken together, the pastoral charge and benediction entrust God's people to heed the summons of the living Word who is already and has been at work in the world. The One who is our Joy continues to be at work in the highways and byways of the world, to which we are enjoined to *en*-joy living life in the presence of the Lord who meets us on life's pilgrimage. Whenever and wherever the living God encounters us in the ministry of Word and sacrament, we are recalibrated to our life's purpose, being strengthened and refocused to the triune God's mission in the world, and in doing so, the commitment to serve and love is not an onerous burden but rather one in which we experience again and again the restoration of joy of God's salvation. Our culture associates "joy" with "happiness," with lounging in a hammock poolside or in the forest. While for a moment

---

10. Presbyterian Church (U.S.A.), *Book of Common Worship*, 82.

it can be that, as our bodies and minds and hearts need Sabbath rest, and certainly I can attest to the power of unplugging for a month and hiking the Camino de Santiago, which brought much joy to my soul, such solitary recalibration is not salutary because our life is not endless caminos and unending beachside margaritas. There's a point where the rest and recovery we receive from recreation is meant to recharge us for the mission that is ahead.

Mark Labberton pointedly raises the question: "What's at stake in worship? Everything."[11] The same goes for the gathered worship of God's people. On this side of heaven, we aren't created to be in the worship service in the sanctuary forever and ever; the time will come when in eternity we will join the heavenly hosts and the communion of saints in endless praise to the living God. On this side, where we long and pray that heaven and earth be one, where "Come, Lord Jesus" (Rev 22:20) is the cry of the saints for deliverance, where we petition the ascended Christ to make his presence and full redemption known in the here but not yet, we continue participating in God's mission, encouraging one another, being inspired and invigorated by the ministrations of the Spirit of Christ who works in and through other people to proclaim the Word, who works through other pilgrims, as it were, to offer testimony of God's oracles, who through other pilgrims will declare the reconciling promise of Christ crucified and risen, who through other pilgrims will reassure us of our identity in God as children born of the water and fed by the Bread of Life and Cup of Salvation, who works through all in all, to the glory and praise of the One who is our Joy, our life's desiring. Alleluia! Amen.

FOR REFLECTION

1. When you consider your life itself as being a worship offering to God, how does that change your disposition?

2. Life as worship is linked to God's shalom vision for transformative justice in the world, which is linked to experiencing joy in God's salvation. What are the work and witness of joy in your life and in the world around you (family, organizations, community, congregation)?

3. Consider the last time you shared with someone or you served someone. Did you experience joy? What was it about that experience that brought joy to your heart—or perhaps didn't?

4. What is God, the One who is our Joy, calling you to be and to do?

---

11. Labberton, *Dangerous Act of Worship*, 188.

PRAYER

Living God, who in Jesus Christ is our Joy and the fountain from which all life flows: we live and move and have our being in you. Far too often we have hoarded your blessings, your gift of salvation, your freedom to ourselves and for the benefit of those whom we think are deserving. Vacate our indifference, our neglect, our self-serving spirit. Free us to live in Christ, to be about his mission for the world, that all will be reconciled to you and one another; and set us on a path to do justice, to love mercy, and to walk humbly with you. Amen.

EPILOGUE

We live to worship the living God, who is the source and embodiment of joy, and because he is our Joy we seek to follow the Lord's will and ways. That means seeking the healing and reconciliation of the world.

This book has been a pilgrimage in itself, born from real struggle and hardship because of being unmoored from my first Love, my Joy. It's a call to be aware, beware, and be alert because it can happen to anyone, to fall into a despair where only the One who knows the secrets of the heart can perceive the pain and the joy that is missing.

When Daniel and I had completed the part of our life's pilgrimage called the Camino de Santiago, Grace and I traveled with Daniel to Davidson College and helped to move him into his dorm. We worshipped with the good saints of Davidson College Presbyterian Church and met some of his new classmates. As we prepared to leave him for the airport, I said to him: "Now our camino journey ends here. Your camino, your camino begins here. And we are here to support you and accompany you." With that, our eldest, who does not wear his emotions on his sleeves, teared up on my chest, and I on his head, as my wife and I embraced him, kissed him, and bade him farewell.

We repeated this goodbye ritual when we blessed our youngest son, Andrew, two years later. We as a family prayed for him in the parking lot of Loyola Marymount University after helping him move into his dorm. He, also, begins his pilgrimage as a young man, whom we entrust to the Living Joy to accompany him every moment of his life.

In this book, I wanted to set out what I experienced in my own wrestling with God and myself, a wrestling that has resulted in a recommitment to life—and not just any life, but a new life, a life of joy, a purposeful life of knowing who I am and whose I am, along with the profound calling that you and I have been given this season of eternity called life for worship, with joy, for the sake of God's transformative justice in the world. When

God reveals God's self to us, as Christ shows us what the kingdom of God is about, freeing us by the power of the cross and the resurrection freedom that burst forth from the empty tomb, such divinely restored agency means that our life is repurposed and reordered for God's purposes, in God's heart.

Our souls rejoice when we are linked to the One who rejoices whenever a human being turns away from their pride and brokenness and trusts in the Lord. God rejoices when the captive is set free, when the naked are clothed, when stranger loves stranger, when neighbor sets the table for the refugee, when the single parent is listened to and cared for, when a child is educated and given a chance to succeed, when an older adult is dignified for their continuing contributions to society, when the church is continually on their hands and knees in serving and advocating for the disenfranchised and marginalized. The pilgrimage of our life and faith, then, is being apprenticed in the ways of the Lord through the gifts of God for the people of God; these gifts—community liturgy, baptism, word, Table, benediction—anchor us to the living God who encounters God's gathered people in holy worship and patterns our living when we are the sent people to live out faith in the world.

There is no greater joy than when the entirety of our life is regarded as lifelong worship for the sake of God's transformative justice in the world; such a disposition towards life, vocation, purpose, relationships, and every part of our existence restores joy to our being and doing—and makes glad the One who is our Joy.

BIBLIOGRAPHY

Andrews, David. "The Lord's Table, the World's Hunger." In *Liturgy and Justice: To Worship God in Spirit and Truth*, edited by Anne Y. Koester, 63–73. Collegeville, MN: Liturgical, 2002.

Blinken, Antony J. "Secretary Blinken Participates in an Aspen Security Forum Fireside Chat." YouTube, July 19, 2024. Interview by Mary Louise Kelly. https://www.youtube.com/watch?v=N9mJIc4zaoE.

Bostrom, Kathleen Long, and Peter Graystone. *99 Things to Do Between Here and Heaven*. Louisville: Westminster John Knox, 2009.

Calvin, John. *Institutes of the Christian Religion*. CCEL, 1845. Translated by Henry Beveridge. https://www.ccel.org/ccel/calvin/institutes.

Carvalhaes, Cláudio. *Eucharist and Globalization: Redrawing the Borders of Eucharistic Hospitality*. Eugene, OR: Pickwick, 2013.

Dostoyevsky, Fyodor. *The Brothers Karamazov*. Translated by Constance Garnett. New York: Lowell, 2009. https://www.gutenberg.org/files/28054/old/28054-pdf.

Everhard, Matthew V. *A Theology of Joy: Jonathan Edwards and Eternal Happiness in the Holy Trinity*. Middletown, DE: JE Society, 2018.

Fagerberg, David W. *Liturgical Mysticism*. Steubenville, OH: Emmaus Academic, 2019.

Galloway, John, Jr. *Ministry Loves Company: A Survival Guide for Pastors*. Louisville: Westminster John Knox, 2003.

Gorrell, Angela Williams. *The Gravity of Joy: A Story of Being Lost and Found*. Grand Rapids: Eerdmans, 2021.

Granberg-Michaelson, Wesley. *Without Oars: Casting Off Into a Life of Pilgrimage*. Minneapolis: Broadleaf, 2020.

Harari, Yuval Noah. *21 Lessons for the 21st Century*. New York: Random House, 2018.

Hunsinger, George. *The Eucharist and Ecumenism: Let Us Keep the Feast*. Current Issues in Theology. New York: Cambridge University Press, 2008.

Klotz, Anthony C., and Mark C. Bolino. "When Quiet Quitting Is Worse Than the Real Thing." *Harvard Business Review*, September 15, 2022. https://hbr.org/2022/09/when-quiet-quitting-is-worse-than-the-real-thing.

Labberton, Mark. *The Dangerous Act of Worship: Living God's Call to Justice*. Downers Grove, IL: IVP, 2007.

Lang, Paul H. *The Pilgrim's Compass: Finding and Following the God We Seek*. Louisville: Westminster John Knox, 2019.

Lewis, C. S. *Surprised by Joy: The Shape of My Early Life*. New York: Harcourt Brace & Company, 1955.

Mathewes, Charles. "Toward a Theology of Joy." In *Joy and Human Flourishing: Essays on Theology, Culture, and the Good Life*, edited by Miroslav Volf and Justin E. Crisp, 63–96. Minneapolis: Fortress, 2015.

Moltmann, Jürgen. *Theology of Joy*. London: SCM, 1973.

Moschella, Mary Clark. *Caring for Joy: Narrative, Theology, and Practice*. Theology in Practice 1. Boston: Brill, 2016.

———. "Elements of Joy in Lived Practices of Care." In *Joy and Human Flourishing: Essays on Theology, Culture, and the Good Life*, edited by Miroslav Volf and Justin E. Crisp, 97–126. Minneapolis: Fortress, 2015.

Office of the General Assembly. *The Constitution of the Presbyterian Church (U.S.A.), Part I, Book of Confessions*. Louisville: Office of the General Assembly, 2016.

———. *The Constitution of the Presbyterian Church (U.S.A.), Part II, Book of Order 2015–2017*. Louisville: Office of the General Assembly, 2015. https://s3.amazonaws.com/newmedia.zpc.org/uploaded/b/0e5891521_1486126485_book-of-order-2015-2017.pdf.

———. *The Constitution of the Presbyterian Church (U.S.A.), Part II, Book of Order 2019–2023*. Louisville: Office of the General Assembly, 2019. https://www.pcusa.org/site_media/media/uploads/oga/pdf/2019-23-boo-elec_010621.pdf.

Pfatteicher, Philip H. *Liturgical Spirituality*. Valley Forge, PA: Trinity International, 1997.

Presa, Neal. D. *Ascension Theology and Habakkuk: Reformed Ecclesiology in Filipino American Perspective*. Edited by Grace Ji-Sun Kim and Joseph Cheah. Asian American Christianity in Diaspora. New York: Palgrave MacMillan, 2018.

———. "From the Board Chair." In *Sustaining Hope: Annual Report 2020*, by Presbyterian Foundation, 11. Jeffersonville, IN: Presbyterian Foundation, 2020. https://issuu.com/presbyterianfoundation/docs/2020_ar_final.

———. "Stewardship of Mind: The Ascension and Our Life Together." In *Beyond the Offering Plate: A Holistic Approach to Stewardship*, edited by Adam J. Copeland, 138–50. Louisville: Westminster John Knox, 2017.

Presbyterian Church (U.S.A.), The. *Book of Common Worship*. Louisville: Westminster John Knox, 1993.

———. *Book of Common Worship: Daily Prayer*. Louisville: Westminster John Knox, 2018.

Schmemann, Alexander. *For the Life of the World: Sacraments and Orthodoxy*. Repr., Crestwood, NY: St. Vladimir's Seminary Press, 2004.

Soerens, Tim. "Subverting Two-Pocket Thinking with Public Joy." *Comment*, January 6, 2022. https://comment.org/subverting-two-pocket-thinking-with-public-joy/.

Stookey, Laurence Hull. *Baptism: Christ's Act in the Church*. Nashville: Abingdon, 1982.

———. *Eucharist: Christ's Feast with the Church*. Nashville: Abingdon, 1993.

Taylor, Porter C. "A Liturgy During a Pandemic." Porter C. Taylor, 2020. https://porterctaylordotcom.files.wordpress.com/2020/03/a-liturgy-during-a-pandemic-pct.pdf.

Watts, Isaac. "Joy to the World." Hymnary, 1719. https://hymnary.org/text/joy_to_the_world_the_lord_is_come.

Wayman, Benjamin. "Rowan Williams: Theological Education Is for Everyone." *Christianity Today*, August 19, 2020. https://www.christianitytoday.com/ct/2020/august-web-only/rowan-williams-theological-education-for-everyone.html.

Zemeckis, Robert, dir. *Cast Away*. Los Angeles: 20th Century Fox, 2000.

Made in the USA
Columbia, SC
25 June 2025